# ECONOMIC RECONSTRUCTION

## REPORT OF THE
## COLUMBIA UNIVERSITY COMMISSION

# ECONOMIC RECONSTRUCTION

### REPORT OF THE
### COLUMBIA UNIVERSITY
### COMMISSION

NEW YORK: MORNINGSIDE HEIGHTS
## COLUMBIA UNIVERSITY PRESS
M·CM·XXXIV

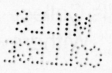

# PREFACE

In his Annual Report for the year 1932 President Nicholas Murray Butler called attention to the "new opportunity for university service" created by the economic and social problems which were sorely besetting the civilized world and which presented a peculiar challenge to those scholars who devote themselves to the fields of study within which these problems have emerged. That there was a prophetic note in this pronouncement the response of the universities to the call for service has in the intervening period amply demonstrated. The relevant portion of President Butler's Report follows.

### New Opportunity for University Service

The years through which we are passing have brought into new and unexampled prominence a series of difficult problems whose solution affects the happiness and satisfaction of the whole world. These problems demand with the utmost urgency study by the very best intelligence which our time can provide. They summon this University to a high task of interpretation and exposition on a scale that has perhaps never been reached. So rapid, so incessant, and so cumulative have been the changes going on in the economic, political and social structure of our modern civilization that they find us not only wholly unprepared to deal with the grave emergencies which they so constantly present to us, but even unable clearly and fully to understand their essential character. To find a way out of these economic and social dilemmas, with their serious and often distressing consequences, is a responsibility which rests peculiarly on the universities of the world, and in high degree upon Columbia University. It is pathetic that with problems of this kind confronting and perplexing men, some of the great funds which have been established by private benefaction for the service of the public are literally wasting the sums at their disposal by scattering them in relatively small amounts over fifty, over a hundred, different and usually unimportant fields of endeavor. These same sums, concentrated in large amounts on one, two, or three of the commanding problems of our time, might well justify in the public mind any fortune, however great, which our economic and industrial system has made possible in past years. However this may be, the duty and the opportunity of this University are obvious.

No one of these problems is more urgent than that which is usually summed up in the phrase: Poverty in the midst of plenty. In this regard our own time reveals a contrast truly ironic and of a kind and extent never before witnessed in the world. This is the contrast between a technological and industrial development which offers for the first time in human history a universal standard of economic well-being and on the other hand an economic mechanism of exchange which seems to defeat, or at least to be unable to make good, that promise of satisfaction and prosperity. The question as to the relation of the consumer's demand to productive capacity is one which has gained increasing attention in late years, particularly since the end of the Great War, and to-day it is paramount in the economic situation which confronts us on every hand. Overflowing barns and impoverished farmers, surplus of raw materials and idle plants, new triumphs of technological skill and new multitudes of unemployed workers, all these point to some fundamental failure of that plan which seeks to adjust demand with supply through the ordinary medium of prices. This is itself a technical problem, since on the one hand all the elements of productive efficiency are present and anxious to coöperate, while on the other hand the human need for the products of this coöperative efficiency is imperative and universal.

The nature of the problem will be better understood if one recalls the elementary fact that all exchange is mediated barter. By progressive stages, as society increased in complexity and in specialized activity, the world passed from what may be called a simple barter economy, through commodity money, the direct use of the precious metals, and standardized metallic currencies, to the elaborate and varied systems of credit or fiduciary money which, with whatever reserves of a precious metal, are controlled by governments and by banks all over the world. In past years these developments went forward through gradual adaptation to conditions which changed relatively slowly. To-day, however, the process of change is so rapid that such farther adaptations as are quickly necessary can only be proposed, explained and brought about by the deliberate concentration upon them of the best constructive thought of the world. How absolutely necessary this has become may be judged from the fact that in the present economic blockade return has even been made, in some parts of the world, back to the ancient and once obsolete system of direct barter.

The problem which presses upon us can be more simply stated through separation from a multitude of complications, some national and some international, which have certainly worked together to create the disasters and maladjustments from which the world now suffers. This problem is not, for example, to be in any way identified with that of the so-called business cycle, though we may confidently expect that to solve it would help mightily in the control of the ordinary fluctuations of economic prosperity. Nor is the problem one which can be met by direct recourse to any of the competing economic philosophies of society, whether those which are based on that liberty which has made possible the accumulation of capital or those which are in whole or in part the outgrowth of the tenets of socialism. The essential point is that two parts of our economic mechanism, the technique of production and the technique of exchange, have evolved, not in interdependence but in semi-independence each of the other, with the result that they do not function in harmony for the service of society. This is a fundamental problem which did not come into being with the present world-wide depression, and it is not one which will be solved by the passing of that depression. One aspect of it has been strongly emphasized by a group of engineers who, impressed by the recent quickening of productivity and the enormous new possibilities which still lie ahead of us in this field, urge the desirability of an entirely new system of control which they term Technocracy. Without accepting their inferences, the data which they are accumulating regarding the efficiency of modern production and its methods will have to be taken into account in any serious study of this whole question.

Columbia University, so far as its resources will permit, should lead in an attack upon this problem. The trained competence and the high imagination of our wisest scholars should be given opportunity to fix their attention on these matters and the challenges of our changing civilization which accompany them. They now occupy the center point of the field of human interest.

The subjects to be attacked are not so much material for meticulous research of the traditional kind as for rigorous philosophic and economic analysis and for the wise and constructive formulation of policy. It would be an act worthy of Columbia University, and one with the greatest potentiality of public service, were it now possible to form a group, composed in part of members of the University staff and in part of others outside our ranks, to attack this problem without delay, in the confident expectation that they would be able, in coöperation, to think this question through and to offer some firm and sound ground on which its solution could be built. The specific task to be entrusted to such a group, which in its conferences would naturally desire to establish fruitful contacts with leaders of finance and industry in this and other lands, would be to examine into and to report upon the adequacy of the existing price and credit system to serve the needs of the twentieth-century community under the conditions which modern technological methods and their application to modern industry have created. This may truly be said to be the fundamental question before the world to-day. Columbia University, with its high prestige and its great and many-sided company of scholars, should be put in position to attack it without a moment's unnecessary delay. Material things can wait; men cannot, and sometimes will not.

In furtherance of this program President Butler brought together a group, very representative in that it included, in addition to various members of the Columbia University staff, some leading economists from other universities and also some students of the problems under consideration whose work lay outside the academic field. In his letter to the Chairman of the Committee President Butler set out its scope and function as follows:

COLUMBIA UNIVERSITY

IN THE CITY OF NEW YORK

PRESIDENT'S ROOM

December 28, 1932

Professor Robert M. MacIver
Department of Sociology

My dear Professor MacIver

I ask your kind attention to the discussion with the title, "New Opportunity for University Service", contained in my Annual Report as President of Columbia University for the year 1932.

It has been made possible for the University to go forward promptly with the proposed intensive study there described. It gives me great pleasure to invite you to serve as Chairman of a group of representative scholars, not all of whom are directly associated with Columbia University, to undertake the proposed inquiry. This group, when constituted, will be at liberty to formulate its own program but among the topics which it is suggested should have consideration are these:

1. Analysis of the part played by the price system in the direction of production

2. Analysis of the fluctuating relationships of income, investment, and consumption within the present price system

3. Examination of price controls to maintain stability (a) of internal prices and (b) of international exchange parities in periods of industrial expansion and retraction

4. Examination of the adequacy of present monetary systems under modern industrial conditions

5. Examination of the economic consequences of improvements in productive technique

6. Formulation of consequent policies.

The consideration which is sought is really very intensive and very intimate. It will perhaps be found that if the members of this group can first spend a few days together either in New York or at some convenient place elsewhere, they might through an intimate meeting of minds accomplish much more and better organize their subsequent work than would be possible either by correspondence or by casual discussion . . . [Here follows the list of members given on p. xii.]

May I express the hope that you will find it possible and convenient to proceed promptly with the organization of this undertaking. It is my belief that a most striking public service can be rendered just now by focussing the thought and the experience of so representative a group as has just been named upon the outstanding economic and social problems of our time.

Faithfully yours,

(Signed) NICHOLAS MURRAY BUTLER

The depression was at its deepest when the Committee began its labors in the first months of 1933. Then followed the banking holiday and the departure of the United States from the gold standard. In rapid succession thereafter came the drastic and far-reaching measures of the "new deal." To take cognizance of these historic changes the program of the Committee had to be continually readjusted. Many of the members became engaged in activities directly or indirectly connected with the plans of the new administration. Three of them came to occupy positions of responsibility which involved their withdrawal from the work

of the Committee. Those who were able to continue with
it gradually arrived, after much discussion and delibera-
tion, at the considerable degree of consensus which made
possible this report.

COLUMBIA UNIVERSITY                     ROBERT M. MacIver
    FEBRUARY 1, 1934

# LETTER OF TRANSMITTAL

January 31, 1934

President Nicholas Murray Butler
Columbia University

My dear Mr. President:

I have the honor to present to you the accompanying report which embodies the conclusions of the Commission appointed by you under date of December 29, 1932. It was a somewhat novel experiment which you undertook in bringing together with members of our own Columbia staff a number of economists from other universities and some other gentlemen whose special attainments qualified them to assist in our deliberations. Consequently, we formed a group representative of many diverse points of approach to the large and difficult social economic problem under consideration, the focus of which was the relation between the technological factors of productivity and the economic conditions under which they operate and which seem at various points to limit their effectiveness. I am happy to state that in spite of the difficulties of the problem and the diversities of approach, a very considerable degree of consensus was attained, the results of which are embodied in the report. The problem is so far ranging that only certain aspects could be included in our survey but I venture to think that in respect of these we have done something to clarify the issues involved and to suggest some practical steps towards their solution.

Owing to other engrossments, some of the members nominated by you were unable to take part in the work of the Commission, while some of those who actively assisted in our earlier deliberations found it necessary to withdraw at a later stage. Chief among the reasons for such abstentions were the tasks and responsibilities which fell to those members who have been participating in activities connected with the program of the present administration. We particularly regretted the loss of their services, though realizing that they were thereby devoting themselves more directly to the same ends which your Commission was seeking to further. The remaining members have given unsparingly of the time at their disposal to the work upon which we have been engaged and have shown a readiness to coöperate in the midst of their other activities which has been most gratifying and which alone has made possible the production of this report.

Faithfully yours,

(Signed) R. M. MacIver

## LIST OF MEMBERS OF THE
## COLUMBIA COMMISSION

Robert M. MacIver, *chairman*, Lieber Professor of Political Philosophy and Sociology in Barnard College, Columbia University.

Benjamin M. Anderson, Jr., Economist of The Chase National Bank, New York.

James W. Angell, Professor of Economics, Columbia University.

Joseph W. Barker, Dean of the School of Engineering, Columbia University.

Adolf A. Berle, Jr., Associate Professor of Law, Columbia University.

John M. Clark, Professor of Economics, Columbia University.

Arthur D. Gayer, *executive secretary*, Lecturer in Economics, Barnard College, Columbia University.

Alvin H. Hansen, Professor of Economics, University of Minnesota.

Alvin Johnson, Director of The New School for Social Research, New York.

Wesley C. Mitchell, Professor of Economics, Columbia University.

Harlow S. Person, Director, The Taylor Society, New York.

James H. Rogers, Sterling Professor of Political Economy, Yale University.

Josef A. Schumpeter, Professor of Economics, Harvard University.

George H. Soule, Director-at-large of The National Bureau of Economic Research, New York.

Jacob Viner, Professor of Economics, University of Chicago.

Leo Wolman, Professor of Economics, Columbia University.

———

The following members found it necessary to withdraw soon after the appointment of the Commission because of the pressure of other work:

Edmund E. Day      Walter Lippmann

The following members were unable to participate in the later deliberations of the Commission by reason of their duties in connection with their services for the National Government:

Adolf A. Berle      James H. Rogers      Leo Wolman

The following member was unable to participate in the work of the Commission after June 1933 by reason of his absence from the United States:

Jacob Viner

The following member resigned from the Commission at a late stage in our deliberations. He did not participate in the preparation of the final form of the report and therefore has no responsibility for any views expressed in it:

Benjamin M. Anderson, Jr.

# CONTENTS

The report falls into two divisions: a General Report prepared as a result of the deliberations of the Commission as a whole; and a series of Special Reports prepared and signed by individual members or sub-committees, supplementary to the General Report.

## GENERAL REPORT

## SPECIAL REPORTS

# GENERAL REPORT

# I. INTRODUCTION

In his letter of invitation to the members of the Commission President Butler directed our attention to a series of closely-bound economic problems of a very challenging nature. To quote from the original letter, among the topics which it is suggested should have consideration are such as the following:

1. Analysis of the part played by the price system in the direction of production
2. Analysis of the fluctuating relationships of income, investment, and consumption within the present price system
3. Examination of price-controls to maintain stability (a) of internal prices, (b) of international exchange parities in periods of industrial expansion and retraction
4. Examination of the adequacy of present monetary systems under modern industrial conditions
5. Examination of the economic consequences of improvements in productive technique
6. Formulation of consequent policies

The central theme, as we have taken it, is that of the adequacy of our present economic order to adjust the economic factors of effective demand or purchasing power to the technological factors of the present and potential capacity of production. In the unparalleled depression of the past four years the question of the translation of the wealth-producing capacity of modern industry and agriculture into the substance of an attainable standard of living has attracted universal attention. The contrast between the advance of our productive powers and the recent decline in economic well-being has thrown into tragic relief a problem which is indeed greatly intensified in times of depression, but which must be examined in the larger context of the general relation of the monetary to the productive mechanism of present-day society. This is so vast a subject that the most we could hope to do was to set out the nature of the issues involved, to follow such leads as seemed capable of exploration within a relatively brief time, to suggest the aspects of the subject which need more prolonged study and research, to draw some tentative conclusions from an analysis of the data at our command, and to formulate some considerations which we submit should guide the policy of governmental and other agencies in so far as they are capable of controlling either the causes or the consequences of the economic maladjustments from which we have been suffering.

The problems with which we deal in this Report are in part subjects of current controversy, in part subjects on which, since they first attracted attention, economists have held divergent views. A complete solution of them, as a purely scientific problem, would not be possible apart from long and intensive research and experiment, if indeed it is possible at all. What alone justifies us in putting forward the statement which follows is that questions of practical policy are involved, the decision of which cannot await the tardy processes of scientific demonstration. Such questions call for the best judgment we can offer, conscious as we are of the many and great uncertainties which still surround them.

## II. PRODUCTIVE CAPACITY AND THE
## ECONOMIC SYSTEM

### 1. *Production versus Productivity*

Regarding our task as that of investigating the responsiveness to productive capacity of our economic system, including the institutions which determine the volume of money and credit in general as well as those which are specifically concerned with the financing of industrial development, we first directed our attention to the claims made by engineers and business experts that the actual output of industry is greatly inferior to that which modern techniques and inventions make possible. A famous American economist, Thorstein Veblen, declared in his volume on *The Engineers and the Price System*,

it is an open secret that with a reasonably free hand the production experts would to-day increase the ordinary output of industry by several fold.

This statement was of course made with reference not to a period of unparalleled depression but to the previous period of relative prosperity. Is it a valid statement? If the statement can be substantiated even in degree, then it means that the economic mechanism, as at present constituted or as at present functioning, sets serious limits to the attainment of higher standards of living for our people as a whole. If it is true in any degree, then we must inquire whether the limits in question are inherent in the mechanism or whether they are due to remediable defects of its operation; and if the former, whether there are substantial reasons for supposing that these limits could be avoided, without creating new impediments to prosperity, either by a reconstruction of the present system or by the construction of some alternative kind of economic system. These are questions of vast range and of profound importance on which much economic thinking has been focused and to which any contribution we could hope to make must be very partial and tentative. It is obvious at least that under present conditions the standard of living of large masses of the people is, even in times of relative prosperity and in spite of great advances for considerable groups, deplorably low. It is equally obvious that the fluctuations of productivity, and the economic and social evils and hazards associated with those fluctuations are deplorably and even increasingly high. If, therefore, it can be shown that to any extent the economic mechanism can be made to respond more adequately than at present to the potentialities of production, the demonstration would to that extent point to a solution at the same time of two most urgent problems. The first is that of raising the standard of living for our people as a whole, and especially for the very considerable numbers who, even in the United States and in recent times of "prosperity," were at or below the poverty line. The second is that of mitigating *directly*—that is, apart from the protection which systems of social insurance offer—the perils to worker and employer arising from those enormous fluctuations in production which are in no respect due to changes in productive capacity.

2. *The Judgment of Engineers and of Business Executives on the Gap Between Actual and Potential Production*

Much evidence is cited by engineers to the effect that the actual capacity of production rendered possible by modern techniques and methods is far from being fully exploited. For example, the report on *Waste in Industry* presented by the Committee on Elimination of Waste in Industry of the Federated Engineering Societies (New York, 1921) dealt with a series of impediments to productivity, both in industrial plants and in whole industries, which included such factors as faulty management, interruptions and restrictions of production, overextension of plant capacity, sales policies (price cutting, cancellations, etc.), competitive wastes in selling and advertising, lack of research, lack of technical eduction in designing and operating, labor turnover, and so forth. The waste (or failure to make effective use of the factors involved in production as judged by the best standards in actual use) was computed as running, out of a theoretical maximum possible of 100 points, from 29 points in the metal trades to 64 points in the men's clothing industry.

The above-mentioned study was of course made from a purely engineering standpoint, and important sources of waste that fall into other categories, such as the lack of information of the consumer regarding the qualities of products, might perhaps be added. Again, some evidence has been adduced which suggests that financial and other vested interests have at times interfered with the promotion and application of new inventions and techniques, even though the economic motive has been regarded as the main incentive to technical progress. Moreover, apart from the waste of productivity due to the various obstacles referred to above, there is the vast loss of productivity due to the large recessions of business activity below the level of the period of maximum prosperity. We may in fact distinguish two major sources of economic waste, one directly associated with the productive process itself, the other inherent in the economic conditions which control the general volume of productive output. These two major sources are not wholly independent of one another, but we should distinguish the problem of waste which is primarily technological from that which is primarily economic.

Since, however, it might be contended that the loss of productivity protested by engineers did not make allowance for the limiting factors inherent in the economic system itself—for competitive conditions as between plants or industries, for the elasticity of demand for products, for the effect of increased production in one plant or industry on the market and resources available to other plants, for the repercussions of an all-round enhanced output on the cost of raw materials, on labor and management, and so forth—your Commission decided to seek the coöperation of some leading engineers in a further survey. A subcommittee, consisting of Dr. H. S. Person, Professor W. C. Mitchell, and Dean J. W. Barker, approached a group of engineers and secured their cordial assistance. Then a questionnaire was sent to 91 prominent engineers, of whom 34 responded by answering the questions. A similar questionnaire was sent to 93 prominent industrial executives, of whom 25 similarly responded. The report of the subcommittee is presented as Special Report 1. Although returns were received from only 42 per cent of the engineers and 27 per cent of the executives, the very high agreement between the engineers as a group, and even more between the engineers and the executives, makes, in view of their leading positions in their respective callings, an important testimony. It undoubtedly expresses the considered judgment of men highly qualified to judge. When we find, for example, that in answer to the question:

What per cent of increase could be effected by the industry reported if equipment and management were brought up to the level of the best current standard?

the mean estimate of the engineers is 90.1 per cent and of the executives 84.4 per cent, we have a very serious challenge to existing conditions which the economist cannot ignore. Perhaps even more remarkable is the fact that in answer to the question:

How much could the output of all industries be increased with equipment and management brought to the level of best current practice?

the mean estimate of the engineering group is 77.6 per cent.

These results are further supported by special studies which have recently been made, such as the Alford-Hannum study referred to in Special Report I.

### 3. *The Economic Problem Raised by the Disparity Between Actual and Potential Production*

We see here a problem of immense significance. It is clear that if our society could continuously utilize to the full the productive capacity which is actually available it could thereby overcome the evils alike of poverty and unemployment, assuming an equitable distribution of national income. What happened during the War, when the volume of goods, taking war and peace products together, increased at the very time when millions of the younger and more vigorous workers were withdrawn from productive functions, is an indication, highly peculiar though conditions then were, of the manner in which potential productivity lies unutilized in normal times. Clearly it is not a physical obstacle, not the "niggardliness of nature," nor yet the lack of inventive capacity or of industry on the part of man, which stands in the way of a much higher and much less precarious standard of living than any people has yet enjoyed. The challenge to the economist is obvious, for engineers and executives alike find that economic factors directly and indirectly play a large part in limiting technical efficiency. This is seen in their answer to Question 1:

If assured a ready market for all goods produced, could the industry reported exceed the best previous record in man-hour output?

to which 70 out of the 71 respondents replied in the affirmative. It is seen more fully in the answers to Questions 4a and 4b, where "lack of effective consumer demand" or "lack of purchasing power" easily heads the list among the economic factors which have, according to the judgment of the respondents, limited the volume of output "in recent years of active trade (1923-1929)," both for particular industries and for industry at large. It is noticeable that competitive and speculative conditions are also given a prominent place in the list.

Here then we have a consensus of professional opinion to the effect that the economic mechanism is not so geared to the productive mechanism as to make fully available for the satisfaction of human wants the powers which industrial and technological development have placed at our command. On this point the conclusions of our subcommittee are very suggestive. They point out:

If we accept the judgment of these fifty-nine engineers and executives that from the viewpoint of engineering technology the productivity of industry could be greatly increased with existing facilities, were it not for limits to effective demand, interest is turned at once to this matter of effective demand. Experience promptly rejects the hypothesis that demand is restricted because all—or anywhere near all—consumer wants are satisfied. Presumably, therefore, the restriction of demand is caused by ineffectiveness, due to the existence of interfering institutions or the absence of essential institutions, in the functioning of the processes whereby total income flows out to the community and is transformed into purchasing power.

There are various questions which economists will quite properly raise before they are willing to draw any conclusions from the data presented by the engineers. What, for example, are the obstacles which have prevented management and equipment from attaining to the "best current standards"? How is the criterion of such standards itself determined? Is it in terms of the amount of profit, or of the output per man-hour or per machine or per unit of power? How far are the limiting factors to the vast all-round increase which the engineers envisage to be found in physical conditions, such as the quantity of available natural resources, or in the human element, the supply of managerial capacity and the proportion of the different grades of labor capable of high efficiency, or finally in purely economic conditions, particularly the flaws in our system of economic organization? Again, if lack of effective demand was the immediate explanation of the lag of output prior to the depression, and *a fortiori* since 1929, can this lack be in turn explained by excessive prices or excessive costs, by growing maladjustments in production, particularly the lack of harmony between the distribution of long-term investment among different industries and the probable demand for their products, or by maldistribution of the output of industry? Certainly, as regards the last few years, it is sufficiently obvious that our main trouble has not been a physical engineering one but an economic one, complicated, as economic problems are, by psychological and political factors.

There are, in effect, three particular groups of problems which are raised by the evidences before us: (1) problems of immediate recovery measures; (2) problems of long-range measures for the control of industrial fluctuations in the future; (3) problems of policies for the tapping of unused productive powers in good times (*a*) by increasing effective demand; (*b*) by raising the productiveness of backward producers nearer to the standards of the best; (*c*) by raising the standard of the best.

Each group of these problems offers a large field for study as well as a field for action. A fuller analysis of the nature of the long-run problems is presented in the special report by Professor J. M. Clark.[1] But, as the author of that report points out, many of the issues thus raised cannot be adequately considered unless and until we gain a degree of control over industrial fluctuations. As will appear later on, we regard the control of these fluctuations as itself an essential condition of the solution of many of the other problems.

It might be said that in times of depression the question

[1]Special Report II, "Productive Capacity and Effective Demand."

of technical productivity is one of minor importance, since in such times the problem is so obviously one of utilizing the existent and not merely the potential productive capacity. But the situation in times of depression may be regarded from this point of view as an extreme instance of a more permanent problem. In periods of active trade technical efficiency, as measured by man-hour output, grows less rapidly than in periods of depression. On the other hand, in periods of depression the higher man-hour output is attained under conditions which curtail the total volume of output, induce the wastes of cutthroat competition, and involve a formidable increase of unemployment with its attendant evils, including the deterioration of the technical efficiency of the unemployed themselves.

In fact, many of the devices to which recourse is had under the stress of bad times are intrinsically wasteful. Such devices range from the raising of new tariff barriers and other impediments in the way of trade between countries to the deliberate limitation of production and even the physical destruction of goods and crops in order to raise the price of the remainder. These devices are in effect a confession of failure in respect of our present ability to deal with the major problem. If they are necessitated by temporary conditions they nevertheless seek to relieve them by means which still further increase the gap between productive capacity and the actual satisfaction of human wants. The specific conditions to which they are addressed, the under-costs returns to the producer, point not to the general overproduction of commodities, a situation inconceivable so long as the vast majority have incomes which do not correspond with their desires, but to the defects of a system which does not permit the full exchange, through a money medium adequate to this end, of all the goods and services which men supply as producers and wish to utilize as consumers.

Policies already adopted to restrict output, particularly in agriculture, have the disadvantage, at a time when total output has been falling for other reasons, of being an attempt to improve the relative position of one group over against others. The question may well be raised whether the farmers' betterment does not rather depend on the expansion of industrial output. In this connection it is important that the N. R. A. should not develop a permanent policy for the closer regulation of output by each industry in terms of its own particular interest. At all costs we must avoid a situation of competitive restriction of output between industry and agriculture, each seeking to improve its relative position, with consequences similar to those of the tariff wars between nations.

If, as many maintain, the extraordinary extent of the world depression is in part explicable by the accelerated tempo of technical advance, the situation is even more ironical in that the very capacity to produce has retarded the activity of production. Surely the economist can have no more important problem than to investigate the possible improvements of existing economic systems which might permit or stimulate the fuller utilization of the powers of production as well as diminish the present fluctuations of economic activity, and if these do not offer sufficient hope, to canvass the possible alternative systems which may be devised to meet these defects. A conservative contentment with the existing economic mechanism is no more scientific for the economist than a similar attitude would be for the engineer in respect of the mechanisms with which he deals.

"Lack of purchasing power" may seem to each producer the outstanding reason for his inability to use the means of production with full efficiency and, therefore, for the general disparity between potential and actual production. The extent to which this lack of purchasing power can be attributed to deficiences in the monetary system is discussed at length below; but it would be a serious error to conclude that these deficiencies are the sole cause of the present disparity or that the disparity can be entirely remedied by adjustments of the monetary system. It is clear that the tendency present in a competitive system for capital to be allocated to each industry in such amounts that the full output resulting from its use can be sold at prices covering the full costs of production is not fully operative. The rate of interest has failed as a sensitive regulator of investment, and the lack of purchasing power is in fact frequently the obverse of excessive investment. This excess may be due in part to the plant obsolescence arising out of changes in the methods of production; but it more generally arises out of certain broad characteristics of the organization of production that have become increasingly important in recent years. Production involving the use of equipment with long periods of productive life and organization upon a large scale has made the estimation of the proper amount of long-term investment difficult and the correction of over-optimistic investment slow. A tendency for corporate management to desire the expansion of corporate activity (often facilitated by the reservation of profits) and errors in investment, due to the few firms in certain industries and their lack of knowledge of one another's investment plans, make for further inefficiency.

Failure to utilize all equipment supplied out of past savings, because the produce cannot be sold at a price which covers all costs, is not an inevitable, but it is now a practical, accompaniment of lack of harmony between investment and effective demand. The relatively small number of firms makes it impossible for them to ignore the effect of their policy upon the price of the product they sell and upon the prices of rivals. Forced to take into account the effect of changes in their output upon prices, tending to pessimism in their estimates of the extent to which demand will expand in response to a fall in price, and anxious to secure a normal profit upon their capital investment, they tend, in the presence of excessive capacity for production, to avoid price cutting. Price leadership, sharing the market, and more direct attempts to discourage price cutting tend to the maintenance of prices and the restriction of output. In some industries price competition has been so modified that prices have remained unchanged for a number of years. Not only do these changes in the administration of industries diminish the elasticity of the price structure, but they also render it rigid at a point at which resources are not being fully utilized. Rivalry may be diverted into the expansion of investment, freight allowances, advertising, and style and service competition which raise costs toward prices, thus reducing profits without transmitting to purchasers either the benefits from improvements in the technique of production or from past excessive allocations of investment.

During periods such as the present, when a general restriction of purchasing power has occurred, these modifications of competitive behavior, with their incidental tendency to maintain prices, serve to intensify the general restriction of business activity. The trust problem has, in fact, reappeared in a new guise. Firms, often without monopolistic positions in the strict sense, but forced by the large proportion of the market they command to take account of their power to affect the market price both directly and through the reaction of rivals to their own policy, have been forced into conduct partly monopolistic. Even where motivated merely by the desire for normal profits, their policies tend to excessive investment and the stalling of the competitive mechanism for adjusting the excess. The spectacle of the partial unemployment of plants equipped to produce goods for which there is dire need is partly due to these changes in industrial organization; but the only escape, unless the present technique of production is to be abandoned, is by way of a control of the broad lines of production and price policy. The writing into codes under the National Industrial Recovery Act of prohibitions upon sales below cost has opened the path to a modified control; but this power lies at the moment mainly with the code authorities that are permitted to prescribe methods of calculating costs. Where all costs can be covered by smaller sales at higher prices there is a temptation to raise prices and restrict output. If the general standard of living is not to be further reduced by attempts to raise prices by the use of this now openly concentrated power, close supervision of the policies of code authorities and their control by the state by reference to a general policy of maintaining economic equilibrium is necessary.

### 4. *The Recovery Program and National Productivity*

Some aspects of the national recovery program have an important bearing on the problem with which we are here concerned, and the comments which follow are addressed solely to these aspects. As will later appear, we regard economic planning as a great experiment in statecraft which the times demand. This vast and difficult enterprise requires an unusual combination of courage and of caution, of foresight and also of readiness to change those policies which experience shows to be mistaken. Such criticisms as we offer are made in the desire that the experiment should succeed and in the belief that its success depends on the same readiness to profit by trial and error as characterizes the scientific experimenter or the engineer.

The statesman, however, has not the same liberty of action or simplicity of objective as has the engineer. This makes additional caution necessary, lest he be committed too far to lines of policy which, however ineffective or even prejudicial they may prove for the end in view, become harder to retrace the longer they are pursued. The situation is complicated by the fact that the conditions in a time of depression call for action which may speedily relieve immediate or urgent needs but which may be out of harmony with or even opposed to the broader objective of recovery. It is on that account most desirable that the activities designed to promote recovery be distinguished from activities which have some other end, no matter how laudable, in view.

These considerations apply particularly to the activities conducted under the National Recovery Act. In so far as they are designed to prevent undercutting in wages and prices and other competitive practices incompatible with a decent minimum standard of living for the worker, they have a humanitarian justification, but they should be viewed in that light. There should be no attempt to impose such regulations on any broader scale with the idea that they are measures of recovery. There should be no illusion with regard to the fact that a general rise in prices through such measures is not a sign of increasing prosperity. It is the rise of prices reflective of increased demand and increased purchasing power which alone can be associated with the process of recovery. The concomitant illusion that a *deliberate* limitation of output, because it raises prices, helps toward recovery is a still more dangerous fallacy. It is more dangerous because the limitation of output of an individual commodity may be for the advantage of its producers if they can thereby control its price. The abnormal situation of agriculture may justify special and temporary measures along such lines, but it should be fully recognized that they involve a tax on the rest of the community, and above all that an all-round application of this policy would make for general impoverishment and would solve the problem of "poverty in the midst of plenty" by removing the plenty. We have already pointed out the danger inherent in the code-making facilities of the National Recovery Act: that they will be employed for competitive limitation of output at the expense of the present and still more of the future national welfare.

Another aspect of the same danger lies in the tendency toward economic nationalism which accompanies programs for the control of economic conditions within the nation. In full sympathy with a policy of national economic autonomy we wish nevertheless emphatically to dissociate this principle from that of national economic isolation. Neither in this nor in any other sphere does autonomy mean cutting ourselves off from the rest of the world. A self-contained economy is one in which the limitation of output, in respect of those commodities which by reason of comparative advantage would otherwise enter into international trade, is practiced on a national scale. In times of depression there are naturally strong impulses toward the heightening of trade barriers, though since the practice of any one country in this regard is countered by the practice of others, the net gain is apt to be less than nothing. But in so far as we emerge from depression the advantage of a restoration of international trade becomes more obvious. What national economic autonomy requires is not a self-contained system, but one in which trade and tariff relations with other countries are subject to pacts deliberately arranged for mutual advantage and so regulated as not to disorganize national economic policies. But this method has only a limited application, in view of the difficulty of reconciling the diverse interests of the various countries involved, and therefore cannot be a substitute for the simpler method of reducing trade barriers for the general stimulation of trade with other countries.

It is further important that the controls devised to safe-guard the public against any form of economic exploitation should not at the same time be such as check legitimate enterprise and prevent the flow of capital into new pro-ductive investment. The practical cessation of new flota-tions since the Securities Act was passed suggests that its terms need clarification so that the promotion of *bona-fide* new enterprises will not be deterred by obligations which are properly intended to prevent the deliberate and wanton abuse of trust from which the investing public has hereto-fore suffered.

# III. THE PROBLEM OF ECONOMIC EQUILIBRIUM

## 5. *The Nature of Economic Equilibrium*

In so far as the gap between potential and actual productivity is a problem of the adjustment of economic factors, it seems clear that no solution is feasible so long as the relation of these factors to one another varies erratically and at the mercy of uncontrolled forces. So long, for example, as general prices move violently up and down, arbitrarily altering the relation between price and cost factors or between creditor and debtor, any calculated policy aiming at a higher level of productivity is bound to be distorted and continually interrupted. A reasonable stability of the price level is, however, only one of the interrelated conditions of that economic equilibrium in terms of which we can more confidently plan for the fuller and less capricious utilization of the potential prosperity made possible otherwise by advancing technology. This part of our report is therefore devoted to the question of the kind of moving economic equilibrium which is both consistent with the tempo of technological and social change and also a condition of control over present and future economic developments.

It is necessary in discussing economic equilibrium to separate out the situation which would obtain in a closed economy from that which exists in an international system. In the statement which follows economic equilibrium is conceived in terms of a closed economy. It is, of course, clear that in the kind of world in which we are now living this conception is not adequate. It is therefore necessary that special consideration be given also to the question of stability in international relations. This involves, notably, a consideration of the stabilization of those factors which are likely to breed maladjustments in the international balance of payments, thereby causing defects in this balance, strains on the foreign exchanges, and the possibility or probability of a complete breakdown of the international financial machinery. Stabilization in the external sphere would particularly have to concern itself with stability in the international movements of capital, whether long term or short term, with a program which emphasizes the balance which must obtain (if maladjustments are to be prevented) between exports and imports of goods and services; with coöperative international movements to hold international price levels in line, thus making possible a concerted program of monetary, banking, and price policy which will not endanger the established relationships of the various monetary systems. These problems will be considered in due course, though it should be here noted that some settlement of them is a preliminary condition for the attainment and maintenance of internal balance. The problem of internal economic equilibrium is frequently envisaged in too narrow a way. It is by no means a question merely of a stable price level. We shall therefore examine briefly a number of concepts of stabilization, leading up to the type which seems to us most adequate and which provides the clearest principle for a practical policy of planned economic adjustment. These concepts may be classified broadly as follows:

(1) Price stabilization

(2) Income stabilization

(3) Debt-income stabilization

(4) Profit stabilization

(5) A moving income equilibrium with profits stabilized.

(1) *Price stabilization*. Economic equilibrium has been defined by a considerable number of economists in terms of price stabilization. This concept, however, has been

subjected, particularly in recent years, to the most critical and vigorous analysis, the results of which are such that, on the whole, it may now be said that economic equilibrium conceived solely in terms of price stability is no longer generally regarded as adequate by specialists in monetary theory. It is clear that under the cover of stability of any one price level, whether of wholesale prices, cost of living, general price level, or any other special price index which may be used, very serious maladjustments may develop. This was notably instanced by the course of events during the years 1924 to 1928, under relatively stable wholesale prices.

To be sure, a very large part of the disequilibrating forces at work during these years emerged in the international sphere. There were, however, in addition, very serious internal maladjustments which developed, but which at the moment went in large part unnoticed, because of the semblance of equilibrium evidenced by the relative stability of the wholesale price level.

(2) *Income stabilization.* Stabilization of money incomes is a monetary ideal which has been advanced by a number of recent writers. Clearly this concept is an advance in important respects over that of mere price stabilization. If money incomes were, in fact, stabilized, one important source of violent price fluctuations would be eliminated. There would, indeed, develop in a progressive society a downward trend in the price level owing to increased productive efficiency and lower unit costs. But violent fluctuations in the price level would be less likely to occur.

But serious maladjustment may develop even though money incomes are stabilized. Mere income stabilization does not ensure that the productive forces will be properly allocated between consumption goods and capital goods. Indeed, violent shifts might take place in the relative proportion of the income directed into these two fields, of a character which would make for instability. Nor is there any guarantee that income stability will insure equilibrium in the cost-price structure. Conceivably considerable fluctuation in profits might occur even under a condition of income stability. Moreover, a maladjustment might also develop in the debt-income relation under income stability.

(3) *Debt-income stabilization.* It probably needs no elaborate argument to show that this criterion of economic equilibrium, while an important one, is wholly inadequate. Debts in relation to income might be kept well within bounds of the requirements of economic stability; yet other serious maladjustments might develop in the cost-price structure or in the relation of profits to other incomes. Again, there might develop violent shifts in the relation of income to the expenditure on investment goods.

(4) *Profit stabilization.* Profit stabilization as here used is identical with stability in the cost-price structure. If costs are kept in a moving balance in relation to prices, neither abnormal profits nor losses should develop in the national economy as a whole.

Yet under profit stabilization there may develop certain maladjustments. Difficulties could arise because the relation of debts to income might get quite out of balance even though costs as a whole were properly coördinated with changes in income. Moreover, since profit stabilization would not of necessity preclude fluctuations in other incomes, there might well develop important shifts in the relative portion of the income spent on capital goods— shifts of a character which cannot possibly be maintained, but which instead inevitably would give rise to fluctuations in the opposite direction.

(5) *A moving income equilibrium, with profits stabilized.* A more adequate criterion is the moving income equilibrium concept. This implies a combination of two elements: (*a*) balance in the cost-price structure (in other words,

profit stabilization); (b) expanding money incomes of other factors. By this is meant that the trend of these money incomes corresponds closely to the trend of real incomes; in other words, as productivity increases money incomes increase in the same proportion.

One further elaboration is necessary, which is perhaps not adequately covered by the already cumbersome term used above. Not only must profit stability cover a balance in the cost-price structure as a whole, but also one between various groups of factors: debts and income; debt and capitalized prospective profit; consumers' goods and industrial equipment; incomes received and incomes spent. The last-mentioned relation—the relative rates of saving and investment—is of especial importance.

It is clear that our criterion is a very complicated one and that no simple indices are adequate as guides for a program aiming at the maintenance of economic equilibrium. For purposes of control it is necessary that we have in the future adequate profit data and adequate data over the whole cost-price system—debts being one of many important items which must be watched among the various cost items.

Undoubtedly, important new institutional arrangements must be made in order to effect the proper control of these various elements. First and foremost, it is of the utmost importance that a deliberate program be undertaken to promote flexibility in the cost-price structure along the lines that are later discussed in this report. It is no longer possible to expect that laissez faire forces under modern institutional arrangements are adequate to break down cost rigidities. A deliberate, planned effort must be undertaken to make costs more flexible. It is of the greatest interest that the country which has gone the furthest in institutional arrangements for controlling costs—Australia—was also the country which by deliberate forethought and social planning was the most successful in breaking down the rigidities in the cost structure during the great depression, and which by deliberate social control and by the use of established institutional arrangements such as wage boards brought about an equilibrium in the cost-price structure which the countries that relied most heavily upon automatic forces failed to achieve.

### 6. *The Gold Standard and Economic Equilibrium*

Prior to the War, and again prior to the recession, by far the greater portion of the civilized world adhered to some form of monetary system based on gold. Under this system the supply of money and credit, because of the primary statutory requirement that notes in circulation must be redeemed on demand in gold coin or bullion, was limited basically by the reserve of gold held in the vaults of banks or of governments. Whether or not the view held by certain economists, that the secular trend of world prices has reflected the changes in the world's total stock of gold, or the stock of gold available for monetary purposes, is accurate, there is no question that changes in the price level responded to changes, relative to the volume of production and trade, in the volume and velocity of circulation of the means of payment, the supply of which was limited in the last resort by the cost of production of gold. The retention of the gold standard proved, however, under the unusual circumstances which arose out of the War, a matter of increasing difficulty, so that the majority of countries were led or forced to abandon it. Since many of these circumstances still remain, it is at this time particularly important to examine the operation of the gold standard as affecting in recent years the internal economic equilibrium of the countries which adhered to it. The conditions and even the prospects of a restoration of an international gold standard should depend on the manner and degree in which it can be reformed so as to be compatible with internal stability and national economic planning. The following synopsis of facts respecting the operation of the gold standard seem pertinent in this regard.[1]

(1) The gold standard served both an international and an intranational function of regulation. Internationally its chief function has been to assure the countries adhering to it the maintenance of fixed exchange parities. The narrow limits of fluctuation were set by the free international movement of gold. Thus the gold standard maintained for these countries, not indeed a common price level, but internationally a closely equilibrated price-structure. Intranationally its chief function has been to keep the supply of money and credit within certain limits and to make political manipulation of the standard of value more difficult.

(2) The international character of the gold standard, made effective by the free movement of gold, had definite effects on the stability of internal price levels. In fact it assured stable parities of exchange by permitting or creating variations in the level of domestic prices. When, as not infrequently, a conflict occurred between the two objectives—stability of the international exchange value of the currency unit and stability of the internal price level—monetary policy had to be determined, not by the requirements of domestic production and trade, but by the demand and supply conditions of foreign exchange.

(3) Leaving for later consideration the question whether these two objectives can be combined under some modified gold standard or other standard operated under international central bank coöperation, we must here point out that they may often be quite incompatible under the gold standard as hitherto established. The paramount duty of the central bank of a country adhering to the gold standard

[1] See Special Report III, by Dr. Arthur D. Gayer, on statements of fact made categorically in the present section.

has been to maintain its currency at par with gold. In fulfilling this function it could not at the same time independently put into effect measures designed to maintain internal stability. The attempts of various central banks and treasuries since the War to pursue both policies at once or to reconcile them have inevitably broken down.

(4) Any one country on the gold standard can at will pursue a deflationary policy to its heart's content. Since the effect will be the piling up of reserves, it can go along in this direction independently of the rest of the world. But the converse is not true. Any country which embarks on an inflationary policy or attempts to arrest a process of deflation, no matter what its previous accumulation of gold, is subject to the peril of being forced off the gold standard. Recent experience has once again conclusively shown that even abundant gold reserves accumulated in previous periods of prosperity can in these circumstances be rapidly exhausted by sudden nervous withdrawals of foreign short-term balances and a flight of capital, as well as by internal hoarding. In other words, central banking authorities must control the total volume of the media of payments to prevent or correct an adverse balance of trade and check a resultant gold export. If world gold prices are falling, a country has the choice between two and only two courses: to maintain its price level stable above that prevailing abroad at the risk of being forced eventually to abandon the gold base; or to lower its entire internal price and money income structure in line with the fall of world gold prices.

(5) In fulfilling the above-mentioned functions, the operation of the gold standard has nevertheless been by no means purely or simply automatic. This is a point of special importance, since in the controversy over the respective advantages of gold-standard currencies and managed currencies the automatic control exercised by the gold standard

has played a rôle similar to that of the automatic regulation attributed to competition in a free laissez-faire economy. In both cases the claim of the advantage of automatic regulation has been premised on conditions which no longer hold, or at all events which hold in less degree than they formerly did. As central banks developed, they first learned how to maintain exchange stability through discount rate manipulation and control over the internal volume of credit. These practices have been pursued by the Bank of England for perhaps a century. In the United States they came definitely into operation only with the establishment of the Federal Reserve System. Then gradually many central banks have attempted by various means to exercise some control over gold movements without alteration of discount rates, while others have held such large reserves that only exceedingly heavy gold losses have necessitated increased rates. Conversely, almost all central banks have tended to some extent to bottle up gold receipts without permitting them to exert their full influence upon the total volume of the means of payment and the general level of prices.

(6) The automatic element in the operation of the gold standard has diminished under post-War conditions.[2] While, as pointed out in the previous paragraph, some management was needed under pre-War conditions, an increasingly large measure of management, and of a more complex kind, has become necessary since the War. Gold movements have been determined more often than not by changes in interest rates, rather than by relative changes in price levels. Central banks have conducted their operations with regard to domestic price structures in large measure independently of gold flows. In the United States particularly, the connection between the gold reserve and the

[2] See also Special Report IV, "Non-monetary Factors Affecting the Functioning of the Post-War Gold Standard," by Dr. Arthur D. Gayer.

credit superstructure has been increasingly ignored. In the pre-War sense we have not been on the gold standard since the War, despite our ample gold reserves. The influence of gold on prices has been limited by the Federal Reserve's management of currency and credit. To this end the devices of "offsetting" and "sterilizing" were consistently employed. The total volume of the media of payments has been regulated independently of reserves and largely to suit supposed domestic business needs.

But particularly during the depression this regulation, which has in effect sought to counteract or inhibit the automatic operation of the gold standard, has nevertheless been subject to such restraints, confusions, and perils, because of the deflationary pull which the retention of the gold standard still exercised, that it failed to achieve its main ends. Great Britain and the countries which followed her off gold in 1931 were spared the long and agonizing process of devastating deflation to which the United States was subject during the next eighteen months by her desperate attempt to cling to gold at all costs. By this course America precluded any measures directed to the deliberate encouragement of business recovery and to the deliverance, otherwise than by wholesale bankruptcy, of the nation from the morass of unpayable debt which extended further the more the process of deflation advanced.

(7) The conclusion is clear. The so-called gold standard of post-War times has been a system not automatically operative but one involving considerable, if insufficiently effective, management. The choice before us, under existing conditions, does not lie between an automatic regulator of money and a managed currency, with or without a gold basis. We cannot, even if we would, avoid the necessity of control. The only choice concerns the form of control we adopt and the objectives we deem most essential for the determination of its policy.

### 7. The Immediate and the Permanent Desiderata for a
### Monetary System

When an economic system has been shaken and disor-
ganized as ours has been since the onset of the depression,
the immediate needs of reconstruction must be distinguished from the permanent needs of a more stable, enduring, and equitable order. The latter demand prolonged
thought and carefully tested experiment issuing in well
matured policy. The former cannot wait so long; the needs
are too urgent and the situation too menacing. They must
be met in the light of the best judgment at our present disposal. Chances must be taken and quick experiments made.
This is the situation which we still face. The series of recovery measures already developed by the Administration
has been determined by urgent necessities. Whatever their
results, they still leave certain major questions unsettled
regarding the immediate future of the monetary system.
To these we first turn.

We agree with the general principle that a rise in the
general level of both domestic and world prices is highly
desirable though we do not regard this as incompatible
with a reduction, which we consider desirable, in the prices
of some specific goods and services. The alternative would
leave us with the still paralyzing disparity between debts
and incomes. Apart from rising prices for a time there is
little hope of increasing production and trade. The absorption of the vast mass of unemployed and the redemption of
many industries, including the great basic industry of agriculture, are impossible apart from the stimulation of trade
which accompanies and is reflected in rising prices. Moreover, there are exceedingly important social as well as economic reasons why the immediate tendency of prices
should be upward, provided it is accompanied by increasing
business activity. There are deep roots of social trouble in
the violent deflation of the past few years and in the des-

perate plight of debtor classes, a situation which has historically been the nurse of revolution. There may be a question whether the rise in the price level can be expected to occur as the result of natural economic forces or whether it must be deliberately engineered, but of the desirability of the rise there can be no reasonable doubt. In view of what has been said in the previous section regarding the unavoidable control of currency under present monetary conditions, no less than in view of the political and social consequences of laissez faire, we cannot assume that the rise of the price level should be left to automatically operative factors.

The frequent suggestion that the 1926 or 1929 price level should if possible be restored is, however, more than dubious. Since the recession much drastic readjustment has taken place, both through the scaling down of debts and the reduction of monetary wages and salaries. If the 1926 or 1929 price level were restored, these factors would also have to be readjusted upwards. There is also reason for believing that the 1929 price level was too high in the United States because, as a result of unit cost reductions, it fostered the boom by creating excessive and ephemeral profits. Moreover, since 1929, further cost reductions effected through improvements in productive technique as well as through reductions in monetary wages have continued rapidly, as in most previous depressions. No definite figure can be prescribed in advance as the goal at which to aim. This will depend on a complex of factors, prominent among them the relative movements of wages and profits, which in the United States are at the moment quite incalculable. The criterion will be a balanced condition of full normal employment and activity, with costs and receipts in a relation which makes economic enterprise profitable but not excessively so. One such question of expediency concerns the position of export staples. They were outstanding sufferers from the recent slump in world prices, aggravating the difficulty resulting from low prices of things farmers sell compared to prices of things farmers buy. The dollar prices of these export staples rose in response to the depreciation of the dollar on the foreign exchanges, which was much greater than its fall in general domestic purchasing power. Thus they gained through this discrepancy, which will presumably be temporary, and are likely to lose as and if the discrepancy decreases, unless foreign prices for these staples rise in the meantime.

How best to proceed toward the above-mentioned goal is a difficult problem which we shall presently consider. Here we will merely point out two conditions to which any price-raising policy should be subject. In the first place it should stimulate rather than retard the restoration of confidence in the future. All schemes intended to meet emergency situations inevitably produce new disturbance in the process. Sudden and arbitrary changes must if possible be avoided. In the second place, price-raising should not be pursued as an end in itself. It should come as the result of stimulated expenditures which increase business activity, not merely as the result of artificial manipulation of the gold value of the dollar, which creates an atmosphere of apprehension prejudicial to business activity.

Of the permanent desiderata, we regard as paramount the establishment of a standard of value which is not subject to violent fluctuations. Since the War the world has witnessed a series of violent price movements which cannot continue if the economic order we know is to survive in any form at all.

We therefore give priority to internal economic stability over stability of the exchange rate for foreign currencies. The latter is at the same time a genuine desideratum. Instability of exchange is a twofold evil which impedes not only international trade but still more international investment. The benefits to be derived from a revival of international trade would be, in our judgment, very considerable. Nevertheless, the impediments to it which the uncertainties of exchange constitute are often much exaggerated. So long as the trader can protect himself by resort to a free market in forward exchange and has the advantage of stable domestic prices, the difficulty in trading because of exchange fluctuations is not of necessity so very serious. It is also worth while reflecting that the sacrifice of internal stability under the "automatic" gold standard to stability of exchange may be indirectly responsible for some of the very impediments to international trade from which we now suffer. For the United States certainly, if it can be attained, internal stability would appear far the more important in view of the overwhelmingly larger volume of transactions which are upset by internal as against foreign exchange instability.

To sum up this argument. Our primary immediate need, so far as the monetary system is concerned, is a rising price level reflecting an increased volume of business and increased employment, and associated with general confidence in the price-raising methods or impulses. Our primary permanent need is a price system maintaining an approximately steady purchasing power of the dollar over goods. This requirement still leaves open the question whether a *slow* secular trend of prices upward or downward may not be preferable to an *absolutely* stationary equilibrium. The concomitant non-monetary conditions necessary to ensure the preservation of economic balance under such a price policy are indicated below. Of secondary importance, though well worth striving for, if it is compatible with the main desideratum, is some such stability in exchange as the traditional gold standard assured.

## 8. *Steps Toward the Immediate Desideratum*

The uncertainties of the present situation and the impossibility as yet of properly evaluating the measures of economic reconstruction at the moment being put into effect in the United States preclude the detailed examination here. We shall confine our argument to the question of the best means of assuring the immediate objective of a rising price level.

In general, there are two methods by which a higher price level can be deliberately sought. Both are dependent on governmental action. The one is direct, the other indirect. The direct method operates on the monetary system itself. Its most drastic form is that of depreciating the currency by one or more of various devices, such as creating new money *ad hoc*, devaluating the dollar to a fixed quota of its former gold content, establishing a new and broader metallic basis for the issuance of currency, increasing the price of gold by governmental purchases, and so forth. A less drastic form is that of increasing the supply of money, through the banks, provided the country is no longer subject to the controls of the gold standard, by means of a low Federal Reserve rediscount rate supported by security purchases on a lavish scale, thus supplying member banks with cheap money. The indirect method seeks instead to stimulate business activity or to inject new purchasing power by large-scale public capital outlays.

The direct methods are all, though in different degrees, subject to a serious limitation. They can have the desired effect only if they succeed in increasing the demand for credit as well as the supply of it. They must not be expected, simply by themselves, to create bank deposits, to stimulate investment and business enterprise. They may cause drastic and sudden dislocations of the economic structure which more than counteract the immediate flurry of buying in anticipation of higher prices. They may not even succeed in adequately relieving the debtor, though adversely affecting the creditor, unless improving business provides him with more funds to meet his obligations. In short, unless new employment as well as new money is created, it would be better to follow the most direct method of all, which is simply to print greenbacks and hand them out all around! Past experience has repeatedly shown that, in a depression, making borrowing easy or money cheap will not necessarily encourage business activity. Unless effective measures are found to increase purchasing power, and the demand for investment goods, the rise in prices and the stimulation of buying due to the direct methods will be based on nothing more substantial than an ephemeral speculative movement likely to collapse again at any moment.

We therefore advocate the indirect methods, though without implying that direct monetary price-raising methods may not be resorted to, in moderate measure and under careful guidance, as a supplement to the former. Of the indirect methods the most important is a large and well-timed program of public works.[3] The most serious objection to this anti-deflationary measure is removed by the fact that the country is not at present tied to the gold standard. The present situation affords a particularly good opportunity for definite large-scale experiment in this direction. Such experiment, now in being, is justified as a method of diminishing unemployment and its attendant miseries even if it accomplishes no other result.

The objections to this program, and to the efforts of the Administration in this direction, do not seem to us to be well taken. The objection is sometimes raised, for example, that capital raised by public authorities for construction work in depressions merely diverts resources from private industry by raising costs of building and of borrowing, and

[3]See Special Report V, "Monetary Policy and Public Works," by Dr. Arthur D. Gayer.

therefore cannot increase employment. This argument rests upon the fallacious assumption of an inflexible volume of credit and an inflexible supply of construction materials. Since, however, there is usually during depression periods a surplus of idle funds seeking secure investment at attractive returns which private business is unable or unwilling to utilize, funds for financing enlarged public works programs can be raised by creating new bank credits, provided government credit is secure and the demand for bonds elastic. The necessary funds would also partly come from reduced expenditures on direct relief. The further objection that public works expansion entails an increase in taxation equivalent to the expenditure involved rests on a confusion of thought, for business recovery will increase tax receipts without the imposition of new taxes. As regards their effect upon the budget, the answer to the charge that public works expenditures throw it out of balance is that the budget can only be brought into an enduring balance if the national income is increased, and this can come about only through a restoration of business activity. To this end public works should contribute greatly.

With regard to the charge of the wastefulness of such expenditures, it is well to remember the appalling wastage of idle man-power and capital equipment in depressions. Nor is the cost of expanded public works as great as it appears, for if the unemployed are not given work by this means they have to be supported in any event out of public or private funds. The real net direct cost of public works, even if we ignore their indirect stimulating effects, is still much less than it seems, while in addition the community receives something in return for its expenditures. Thus the apparent magnitude of the cost is deceptive. But it is chiefly for their indirect effects in "priming the pump" of economic recovery that large programs of public works in depressions are valuable.

The assertion that a sufficient volume of genuinely needed public works cannot be found in depression periods to give substantial employment we consider quite baseless, though delay in getting it under way at short notice often cannot be avoided in the absence of carefully formulated plans and preparations. During the depression a huge volume of public works has been suspended throughout the country through the wholesale elimination of all possible construction items from numerous local budgets because of the shortage of funds, though this has not been true of the Federal government. Road and bridge building, in particular, is an example of construction work suitable for this purpose, both because it can be put in hand rapidly and entails expenditures which are bound to be made sooner or later. Schemes for slum clearance, the erection of decent workers' dwellings, and city planning projects suffer from the defect that in most cities comprehensive and detailed plans have not existed hitherto, but they offer almost boundless opportunities in the future for construction work of the highest social utility. For this reason prime importance should not be attached to the "self-liquidating" character of projects to be undertaken. On the contrary, since the object of such expenditures is to increase the total volume of purchasing power, the choice of projects should be determined by their social utility rather than by the prospect of a specific income yield accruing from the services to which the projects are devoted.

### 9. *Steps Toward the Permanent Desiderata*

Under any conceivable form of economy, whether capitalist or socialist, a price system is inevitable. The idea that some other kind of unit—of work, energy, physical output—can be *substituted* for a unit of value is mere confusion, since these other units become themselves measures of relative value. Some coefficient of economic choice must exist. This necessity of a price system is sufficiently shown in Special Report VI, by Professor Schumpeter. It is there further shown that, apart from the expression of consumers' preferences, the process of choosing between alternative methods of production requires that values be attributed to the different means of production available, and these again are coefficients of those choices that are expressed as positive acts of production or exchange. When these coefficients of choice, whether of producers or consumers, are expressed in units of money they are called prices, but their essential nature remains unchanged.

It should be noted, however, that there are certain limits to the guidance as between alternatives which a price system provides. Generally, if the cost of producing one thing registers what the productive resources would be worth in producing something else, the first thing should not, apart from some special social utility, be produced unless it will cover this cost. But if the choice lies between producing that thing and standing idle, the same price accounting is no longer a sound guide to the interests of the national economy.

Moreover, the fundamental necessity of a price system has nothing to do with the justification of the particular (and historically recent) form of price system under which our economic activities are at present conducted. It falls in a vital respect far short of the ideal. Above all, it depends on a standard of value subject to violent fluctuations. The disastrous consequences of price instability, in the light of recent experience both at home and abroad, need hardly be dwelt upon. The confusion introduced into economic life and the cruel injuries and injustices inflicted on society by price chaos have often been described in detail. The evil has a twofold aspect. Rapid changes in the price level not only have a calamitous effect upon *productive activity;* but they also arbitrarily alter the *distribution* of national income between different classes of society. In addition they play havoc with smooth economic, and consequently with political relations, not only between classes but also between nations.

We have seen that under the traditional gold standard the internal control of prices is hampered by the necessity of maintaining stability of exchanges with other gold-standard countries. An expansive or restrictive credit policy, independently initiated by any one country, is visited by an excessive gain or loss of gold. Thus, not only does the gold standard permit business fluctuations, it compels all countries adhering to it to participate in them. In depressions this circumstance can easily produce violent destructive liquidation passing far beyond the limits required for the correction of maladjustments. An almost simultaneous competitive raising of bank rates by all gold-standard countries has very different results from the raising of its rate by any one of them singly for the purpose of counteracting a gold outflow. The international money flow is not by the former process changed, but merely slowed down in general, and pressure is put upon internal business and international trade over the whole gold-standard area, as a result of the competitive scramble for gold. The gold standard is likely to work well enough in periods of "normal prosperity," but it permits and even encourages the development of maladjustments on a world-wide scale by spreading the effects of excesses in either direction. In periods of crisis, particularly, it tends, before it breaks, to reinforce rather than alleviate depression.

It does not follow that a reformed gold standard, managed under central bank coöperation, might not be so constructed as to permit a considerable degree of internal control combined with the advantage of a stable exchange. We are here merely pointing out the necessity, under the gold standard as previously operative, of subordinating the

former to the latter when a conflict occurred between the
two objectives. This fact is in our judgment sufficiently important to make a return to the old gold standard undesirable without an assurance of drastic reform through
international coöperation. What these reforms should be
and whether their establishment would justify our return
to gold is a question we shall further examine. Meantime it
suffices to point out that such international coöperation is a
process requiring a difficult preliminary adjustment of
interests. While the advantages to be derived from concerted international action are enormous, while they are of
great importance even apart from their direct economic
benefits, they can in large measure be achieved only
through patient, thorough, and probably slow deliberations, and there is still no guarantee that the necessary
agreement will be forthcoming. It would therefore be
foolish to wait for internal price stability until it can be
achieved by means largely beyond our control. There is
good reason to believe that a preliminary equilibrium can
be achieved without the return to an international standard. After this is achieved it will be easier to plan for a
return to what should be a greatly reformed and internationally managed gold standard.

Monetary equilibrium must be achieved in the not
distant future. The uncertainties and confusions of instability can be endured for a time and may not be too high
a cost for the desideratum of a higher price level. But any
prolonged instability, with the dislocation, uneasiness,
flight of capital, and check on new investment which it
would involve, would have very serious consequences.
Fortunately, while internal stability could not be attained
under the traditional gold standard, this end can be pursued in its absence, while we are waiting for some better
international system. It is an entirely fallacious notion
that paper standards are uncontrollable. It is strange that
such statements should still be made by monetary author-

ities in the light of the experience with paper currencies in the past few years. During the periods when England has been off gold, from 1797 to 1821, from 1914 to 1925, and again since 1931, the paper currency was never abused by inflationary excesses. In fact, in terms of their internal purchasing power, paper currencies have shown themselves far more stable than gold currencies during the last two years, despite the critical difficulties of the times and the grave temptations they offered to governments to indulge in inflationary finance. Between September, 1931 and the banking panic of 1933 it was not the pound sterling, the Canadian dollar, the Scandinavian currencies, etc., which were unstable, but the American dollar, the franc, the mark, and other gold currencies. The paper money of the "sterling area" retained a remarkably steady purchasing power—altogether too steady in the opinion of those who would like to have seen a deliberate expansionist policy adopted to correct the previously deflationary trend of prices—while gold underwent an outrageous appreciation in value.[4]

### 10. *Conditions Under Which a Return to an International Gold Standard Should be Considered*

No reasonable advocate of a return to gold would propose that we simply reëstablish the old order, so long as the conditions under which it broke down are still operative, and so long as certain defects which the order itself has revealed are not remedied. We suggest that the following are the minimum requirements without which it would certainly be preferable to maintain an internal stability on a domestic instead of an international standard.[5]

[4]In various countries respectively on and off gold between September, 1931, when England left the standard, and March, 1933, when we did so, the percentage change in the wholesale commodity price level was as follows (figures of Federal Reserve Bulletin): U. S., —15.5; France, —18; Netherlands, —21; Germany, —17; Canada, —9; England, —1; Sweden, —2; Japan, +18.

[5]See Special Report VII, "Monetary Policy and the Monetary Standard," by Dr. Arthur D. Gayer.

(1) The first and most obvious condition is a satisfactory settlement of the war debts and reparations question, preferably by virtual cancellation, to remove this mischievous factor from interference with the normal current of international trade. Readjustment in certain cases of private debts to prevent defaults will also be necessary.

(2) Second is the reëstablishment of a reasonable degree of freedom in the international flow of goods and services by the removal of the more obnoxious forms of trade barriers. It should, however, be recognized that the reduction of import duties, quotas, etc., is subject to various resistances and that in certain cases such reduction conflicts with policies dictated by internal needs. Our Industrial Recovery Act and Agricultural Adjustment Program may be cited in this connection. The need for a measure of control over the foreign trade of the country in the interests of long-range national plans will make essential the retention of certain trade restrictions.

(3) Third is a general and sufficiently specific undertaking by central banks that in the future management of the gold standard "the rules of the game" will be better observed than in the past, and particularly that gold movements will be permitted to exercise their full influence on the price levels of the countries both losing and receiving gold.

This undertaking, however, would have to be coupled with another measure of coöperation between central banks providing for common policies in the joint management of the gold standard to preserve reasonable stability in the value of gold. Our return to the gold standard on any other terms would be hazardous and might prove most unfortunate. To put this condition into effect agreement will be required among the great powers that such economies in the use of gold will be practiced as will prevent a rise in its purchasing power. The prevention of future gold shortage may quite well require that the stipulations regarding legal reserves now in force be drastically modified or possibly even entirely abolished.

(4) But none of these measures can accomplish much without a previous restoration of more normal activity and employment. A general rise in the world level of wholesale commodity prices and the restoration of equilibrium between prices, wages and debt charges must be effected before a return to a fully international gold standard can be safely considered.

(5) Greater flexibility of many internal factors will be required to insure the successful functioning of the gold standard, but in some respects *less* freedom will be necessary. In particular much more control than hitherto must be exercised over the volume of foreign lending to see that it is brought into harmony with the volume of the foreign balance. There are no grounds for the widespread but naïve belief that these two forces are of necessity automatically equated.

Adherence to an international gold standard is desirable only if these guarantees of its good behavior in the future are secured. Consequently the *immediate* alternatives before us in the quest for economic equilibrium would seem to be as follows:

(1) We can devaluate the dollar around its present foreign exchange gold-value, returning thereby to the international gold standard and seeking by whatever controls we can devise to prevent an excessive impact of international gold movements on our internal equilibrium in the present disturbed state of the world.

(2) We can maintain a reasonably steady price for the dollar in terms of foreign currencies by means of one or other of a number of devices. Under this system the course

of domestic prices would move upwards only in response to internal business developments and the stimulation of government expenditures, not as a result of inflationary manipulation of the currency. One or other alternative is a necessity if we are to avoid the perilous paths of inflation, but the latter alternative would leave us free to determine the conditions on which we finally return to an international gold standard, if and when this step seems safe and advantageous.

In any event the choice before us lies not between a managed and an automatic system. Whatever standard we accept, whether an international or a national one, will require a great deal of management. The advantage of the second alternative is that we can proceed in the meantime to establish a form of internal equilibrium that will not be at the mercy of external developments beyond our control, and can examine without hasty commitment the implications of a truly international system. We can explore the question: how far, for the world as a whole under gold-standard conditions, the inelastic supply of gold is, in spite of economies in its use by various devices, a genuinely restrictive factor on the expansion of credit to meet the needs of expanding production. We can well, before the world is ready for a new order and as an experimental preparation for it, make agreements for tentative cooperation with other price-stabilized, paper-standard countries, such as Great Britain, perhaps by way of a reciprocal acceptance of Treasury Bills in international settlements, or perhaps by an agreement that exchange rates will be allowed to fluctuate only within certain assigned limits. In short, the door is open for safe and fruitful experiment in international coöperation, *once we have attained a sufficient control over unbalanced factors to assure a reasonable degree of national economic equilibrium.*

## 11. *Controls Necessary for the Maintenance of a Moving Economic Equilibrium*

In order to maintain economic equilibrium it is necessary in the first place that the standard of value should be transformed from an erratically fluctuating into a relatively stable one, in the sense of the term explained below; and in the second place that the various factors in the internal cost-price structure should be kept in a harmonious relation to one another. Each of these conditions demands the development and exercise of appropriate controls the nature of which will be presently examined.

First, however, we wish to warn against the mistake of regarding price stability as an absolute inflexible principle in the realization of which the dollar would become as fixed and undeviating a measure of value as the yardstick is a measure of length. Even were this attainable it is more than doubtful whether such an ideal would be desirable. There are considerations that favor a secularly rising price level, other considerations that favor a moderate secular decline. These slow or long-run movements are here not in question. What is without doubt desirable is to prevent the constant and often severe short period fluctuations of the standard of value. This requires the maintenance of a proper balance between saving, consumption, and capital expansion. In the last analysis the consideration of paramount importance is the maintenance within the internal cost-price structure of the right relationship between cost factors and selling prices, one which prevents prices from rising too much above costs or costs from cutting too deeply into profits. There is no especial virtue in any particular price level in itself and for its own sake. The best price level will be the one which best facilitates that mutual adjustment of costs and prices, promptly and with least friction, which is continually necessary in a progressive economy. Under a monetary policy the aim of which was relative stability of prices, the closest and most careful attention would have to be given to the movements and interactions of a large variety of other factors, monetary and non-monetary alike. Experience prior to 1929 clearly demonstrated that violent maladjustments can develop under a relatively stable commodity price level if the behavior of non-monetary factors is not appropriate to such a price level. The ultimate criterion in a system of private enterprise, under which activity is pivoted on profits, must be the movements of the profits index. If unit costs are being steadily reduced as a result of improvements in productive technique or organization, the preservation of economic stability requires either that prices be reduced or that monetary factors of income other than profits be raised proportionately. Otherwise excessive profits will accrue to entrepreneurs and induce capital overexpansion and security inflation which must inevitably result in a reaction that monetary policy is powerless to prevent. For the economic system to function well, profit margins must be adequate but not excessive.

A price level which falls in proportion to unit-cost reductions due to increased economic efficiency, and thus passes on the increased product of industry to consumers in the form of an enhanced purchasing power of their incomes, is not only extremely difficult to secure under the very imperfectly competitive conditions of to-day, but has also certain practical and psychological disadvantages. For example, it would not satisfy in a direct and obvious manner the demands of labor to share the fruits of economic advance. The alternative principle of a relatively stationary price level is preferable in these respects. But this preference is conditional upon the progressive increase in national income which may be expected in an advancing economy being steadily distributed in rising wages and salaries.

Proposals to this end are made below. Such a policy of stabilization thus implies very much more than an attempt to regulate economic activity through monetary control alone. The monetary authorities could never for a moment be indifferent to the behavior of a variety of non-monetary elements. The total picture would have to be kept continuously in mind, and unremitting attention given not only to actual price movements but also to the volume of production, the condition of employment, the movement of wage rates and payrolls, the rate of business earnings, the yield on various types of investment, the volume of new security issues, the demand for credit, the volume of foreign trade and foreign lending, and so forth. Thus, were the *aim* of monetary policy to keep commodity prices relatively stable, the criteria for assessment and for action would be manifold, and the purpose and test of success of the policy would be the preservation of a proper balance between the various elements in the internal cost-price structure.

The *modus operandi* of the alternative policy directed to a price level falling in proportion to costs is not difficult to state in general terms. It would be the maintenance, on the part of the banks, of the total supply of money and credit, not indeed at an absolutely constant and unchanging volume, for changes in the "circuit velocity" of money, and perhaps also in population, would have to be allowed for, but at an amount which with these allowances would be approximately unvarying. The result in that case would be the passing on to the community of the fruits of economic advance not in the form of steadily increasing money incomes, as would be necessary under stable prices, but in a steadily increasing purchasing power over commodities. As between the relative merits of these two alternative courses there is much room for difference of opinion, for one's preference in this regard must of necessity be chiefly a matter of judgment based upon a weighing of imponderables.

Let us suppose, however, that we have secured the practicable desideratum of relative price stability, understood in the terms explained above. It must be remembered that it is only the general level of prices, whether the selected index be that of wholesale prices or any other, and not the prices of particular commodities, which is thus brought under control. The relative advance in technical efficiency of one industry as compared with another will still be reflected, according to the degree in which it is competitive or monopolistic, in relative price reductions or in larger differential gains. The same, of course, would be true of any advantages accruing to an industry through the expansion of demand or other favorable developments. The economic incentive to efficiency will therefore continue to operate. On the other hand, a general advance in efficiency would not reflect itself in a general reduction of prices, since the objective of policy would be to keep the general level stable. There will then be the problem of increasing the rewards of the productive factors which do not receive them automatically through increased profits. It will be necessary that wage rates should increase on the average in proportion to unit-cost reductions. A relatively stable price level will make it possible to calculate these reductions more exactly, given fuller statistical data and proper accounting methods. The principle could be recognized, and machinery might be set up to facilitate this end, that as unit costs decrease average money wages are to be proportionately increased. We recognize, however, that the carrying out of this principle is beset by considerable difficulties.

Such regulated wage and salary increases would mean a constant increase in effective demand for goods in the degree in which industrial advance occurred. The essential problem of control is to adjust wages upward in line with increased productivity lest windfall and excessive profits destroy the economic balance. (In this connection it should be borne in mind that in the United States, in 1929, approximately 67 per cent of retail purchases were made by families receiving incomes of $2000 or less per annum, approximately 80 per cent by those receiving $3000 or less per annum, and approximately 84 per cent by those receiving $5000 or less per annum.) The technical difficulties of regulation would be considerable but they should not be insuperable. The fact that labor would share proportionately and without bitter warfare in the gains of industry would create an entirely new basis for a coöperative spirit in industry.

Problems of adjustment would still remain, many of them difficult enough. The point is, however, that with the great disturbing factor of excessive price instability removed, they should be more manageable than before. After all, it is enormously more difficult to deal with crisis situations after they have developed than to maintain a system which prevents their development.

Under the present order there is no guarantee that the rewards of industry will be distributed in a manner calculated to assure the stability which we have in view. Cost reductions, if the industry achieving them is controlled by price agreements or if there is any considerable degree of monopoly involved, go directly as additional profits to entrepreneurs or capitalists. Even if the workers gain their share it is through strife and concomitant disturbance, while in strongly competitive industries the gain would not be reaped directly by the workers at all, but only indirectly in the degree in which they benefit by price reductions. The rapid increase of profits in the more sheltered industries brings in its train an increase in the demand for producers' goods, an increase in the demand for stocks and bonds, activity on the speculative markets, an increase in the demand for credit for speculative purposes, and an increase in corporate surpluses and reserves, which in turn are devoted to the purchase of producers' goods, purchase of stocks and bonds, and loans to speculators. With the diversion of funds to speculative capital expansion the gains of industry are first locked up and then dissipated in the ensuing depression. Under the projected system the gain would be in some measure safeguarded by a better economic balance. It is true that other disturbing factors would still need to be guarded against, particularly in the relation between saving and investment. But the danger signs would be clear, signs on the one hand of growing unemployment, and on the other of abnormal profits. When these signs appear the appropriate controls could at once be set in motion.

The maintenance of a stable price system, however, would obviously not achieve these ends unless special attention were given to the great variations in price flexibility and rigidity which exist throughout the range of modern industry. It is these rigidities which defeat the presuppositions of a laissez-faire or automatically regulated economy. Since it is not practicable, even were it desirable, to enforce real competition in certain monopolistic and quasi-monopolistic areas, there is no possible solution of the problem they create apart from control. With a relatively stable price system the problem becomes more determinate.

In pursuing this policy a certain amount of planned flexibility can be combined with and would facilitate the aim of planned stability. A considerable measure of flexibility could be achieved by the orderly adjustment of some five or six fundamental cost groups. The following are suggested for consideration: (1) interest charges; (2) depreciation; (3) railroad and public utility rates; (4) basic fuel and metal products; (5) taxes; (6) wage rates.

Much research is available on the precise mechanism by

which adjustments could be made in a number of basic costs. For others additional work needs to be done. But the problem is far from an impossible one if we definitely set ourselves the task of deliberately securing, through systematic planning, an orderly scheme which combines flexibility with stability.

### 12. *Controls Designed to Offset Fluctuations in Purchasing Power*

It is obviously desirable that the goal of internal stability should be attained without undue resort to the policy of increasing or decreasing the supply of money. Other stabilizing factors should be utilized, where otherwise advantageous, which might obviate so far as possible the necessity of this expedient on the part of the central banking authority. We have already suggested that a long-term program of public works would be of considerable service in this direction. A second method may be here suggested, which has, moreover, the inestimable merit that it would more completely insure the working masses against the gravest of all the evils that depression inflicts, that of unemployment.

In recent times of active business, corporations have in limited measure tended to accumulate reserves in order to assure a more steady flow of dividends to their shareholders. This practice, however, has had disturbing consequences because undistributed surpluses have gone into the capital market in greatest quantity in boom periods, thus stimulating investment unduly, while the withdrawal of these reserves in periods of depression has had the opposite defect of retarding the return of investment. It is here suggested that the accumulation of unemployment reserves against times of declining activity would introduce a new element of stability and that the reserves could be so administered that in such times they would mean a genuine new flow of purchasing power to the consumer. As employment diminished, the unemployment reserve funds would be supplied from the banks from the built-up reserves.

The method of administering such reserves, in order to assure that the payments come from idle money or newly created bank credit instead of from the diminished income stream, is a matter of the first importance. Since it requires considerable analysis, it is treated in a special report.[6] The plan suggested would be capable of application to dividend reserves as well as wage reserves. The combination of the two, as consumers' reserves, would constitute an important addition to consumers' purchasing power at the times when producers' credit is most limited. The danger of the exhaustion of such funds would be much reduced by the fact that they are meant to operate in an economy in which a high degree of balance is otherwise assured.

Whether the combination of the two types of reserve fund is feasible or not, assurance against unemployment would not only be most desirable in itself but would be a factor of steadiness in purchasing power when it is most required. In the very act of protecting its citizens against the greatest menace to industrial life the state would in this way be creating another instrument for the control of business fluctuations. In this as in the other aspects of the whole program of stability the state is stepping in to do what private business cannot achieve and what nevertheless is necessary for the common weal and in the last resort for the system of business enterprise itself.

[6]Special Report VIII, "The Flow of Purchasing Power," by Professor Alvin H. Hansen.

## IV. STEPS TOWARD A PLANNED ECONOMY

### 13. *The Meaning of Social-Economic Planning*

While the idea of social-economic planning is entering more and more into the outlook of statesmen, economists, and the public generally, its real nature and the conditions under which it must operate are often not clearly realized.

There are broadly two sets of considerations from which the modern concept of a planned economy has taken form. On the one hand there are considerations arising out of the historical development in which the state has been led to assume new and more constructive tasks of regulation in the economic sphere. Beginning with certain elementary types of safeguard, particularly for women and children in industrial occupations, this regulation extended its scope to include various provisions of social protection and insurance, provisions for the control of monopolistic organizations and agencies, for the conservation of national resources against wasteful exploitation, for the control of banking, currency, and credit, for the assurance of national advantage in certain fields, and so forth. An essential difference between the political order and the economic was that the latter lacked any central agency of coördination and control. Consequently, where competitive conditions were grossly unequal or where competitive conditions were themselves supplanted by monopolistic conditions, the only recourse against consequent exploitations and encroachments seemed to be the state. The same difference has inspired the idea of economic planning, on the ground that the crises, disturbances, and maladjustments arising in the economic system require not only the intervention of the state after they have occurred, but also its deliberate concerted action to prevent their future occurrence and to give stability and direction to the economic life in the interest of the national well-being. Any political activity to this end may be termed economic planning, however limited or however comprehensive it may be.

Obviously, the effective range of such planning depends on the degree to which government can discover and enlist in its councils those most highly qualified for this most difficult task, and can assure that their services shall not be at the mercy of political expediencies. The difficulties here suggested are very great and can be overcome only where the necessity of planning is strongly felt by the people as a whole. Even then it is an undertaking involving some extraordinarily difficult problems. It would be wrong to contrast an ideal scheme for a planned economy with the actual operation of an unplanned economic system. The operation of a planned economy involves trial and error, miscalculations and wastes. The hopeful aspect is that such mistaken experiments can be corrected by experience in a form of enterprise towards which the states of the world seem to be driven by the logic of events.

The second set of considerations from which the idea of economic planning is derived is of a more technical nature. They are, however, particularly important in that they reveal the specific function of economic planning and help us to correct some misleading notions which have come to be associated with this principle. In this aspect the idea of economic planning has been suggested by the extraordinary development of the planning function in the conduct of modern business enterprise. Imagination carries the technique of this individual-enterprise planning over to the plane of national planning.

The reference to the management engineer's concept of planning serves not only to give precision to the principle but also to correct two erroneous ideas frequently present in the discussion of the subject by business men and economists. In one respect too much is attributed to economic planning, in another respect too little. Too much is attributed when it is conceived of as being concerned with the management of every constituent enterprise in an industry and even with details of the internal management of enterprises. Too little when it is pictured as concerned merely with physical production. Planning as it has developed in individual enterprise is concerned just as much with finance, sales, and industrial relations as with the technique of production.

A brief review of the development of the planning function in individual enterprise will show that it is essentially a harmonization of centralized and decentralized operations, aiming to establish a more efficient order with a greater degree of freedom and initiative in specific tasks.

Historically, the planning function was first developed in the production department and in the individual work-place. It set up standards of objective and method for each work-place; but having set up these controlling standards, it immediately freed the workman from the continuous observation and interference of the foreman, which had been necessary before the day of standards. Here was the first step in harmonizing centralization with decentralization—a first step in centralizing environmental control and in decentralizing the details of the work.

The same process was carried over from the individual work-place to the entire shop and from the shop to the entire factory, since planning for the individual unit could not be properly achieved unless it was applied also to the interrelated units. In this way greater freedom over details was assured in turn to foremen and superintendents and a further stage in the harmony of centralization and decentralization was reached. In the process it appeared that the coördination of productive units required also a policy of selection, training, and treatment of workers. It was further discovered that stabilization of the factory required that it be brought into harmony with the conditions of the market and of selling; and then into harmony with the conditions of finance. With each of these steps there was set up a new type of standard of objective and method, but also with each of these steps, and because of the accompanying new standards created, a greater freedom of departmental executive action within the area bounded by the standards was also set up.

It is this development of planning which has made the modern, huge, multiple-plant corporation manageable. In an earlier day, when the chief executive had to be concerned with the direction of details, there was a limit to the size of a plant which could be properly managed. Today there is practically no limit where there has been developed the technique of planning indicated above. Executives have progressively eliminated their concern for details and have progressively concentrated on concern for environmental controls.

The principle of economic planning, carried over to the national sphere, has the same objectives on this grander scale. It seeks to leave a maximum freedom of action within a set of controls designed to keep in harmonious relationship those interdependent economic factors which get out of adjustment with consequences so serious to and so disruptive of the national economy and the national well-being. Thus it aims to establish an equilibrium among all the service factors which accommodate industry. It would regulate, in so far as found desirable to this end, the banking system, the currency system, the system of the creation and allocation of credit. It would regulate the education, training, and employment conditions of labor. It would establish conditions of economic security for workers and define a policy of retirement and old-age allowances. It would set up a research unit which would provide industry

with elaborate data concerning the trends in production of
various commodities for the guidance of individual industries and businesses. It would discover alike the possibility
and the need of a progressive harmony of centralization
through environmental controls with decentralization of
actual management of enterprises, giving more scope to individual initiative. Vast as are the problems involved, it
should be remembered that such planning is in line with
the trend of policy of the modern state and with the demands made upon it; that it has been applied with evident
success in great industrial enterprises (such as General
Motors); that it is a program not for the reduction of initiative but for its preservation and enhancement under the
conditions of an ever more complex and interdependent
social and economic order.

## 14. *The Control of Price Rigidities*

The case for automatic economic regulation assumes that
on the whole the price structure is flexible, that the rigidities which exist are of secondary importance, and that
where they stand in the way of the free functioning of the
system they can be curbed or diminished. In short, its advocates would resort to control only to make control otherwise unnecessary, believing in any event that centralized
or political regulation is less admirable, less competent, and
less effective than the operation of the individualist
"choice of independent producers." The case for deliberate
or planned regulation does not deny that there is an important place for individual choices and incentives and for
the controlling action of competitive factors. It does claim,
however, that whether or not these free choices motivated
by private advantage would in a freely competitive order
yield better social results if released from all public control
—a supposition highly dubious in the light of the history
of industrial development—the premises of this proposition

are destroyed by the realities of present-day economic life
and by the actual trends now in progress and rendered inevitable by technological advance.

In the first place, we have a situation in which the prices
of some commodities, including the basic agricultural
commodities, are exposed to the sweep of world forces,
while others are sheltered in various ways not only from
external influences (by tariffs and other impediments to
competition, effective particularly if the industry is not on
an export basis), but also from internal competitive influences, according to the extent of monopoly or of price
maintenance within the industry. Moreover, the supply of
certain commodities, here again conspicuously those of
agriculture, is not so responsive to price changes, especially
downward, as are others. In the short run the production
of these is apt to be actually increased rather than curtailed
upon a fall of prices, owing to the immobility of the farmer
who makes a desperate effort to meet the increasing burden
of debt charges. In the second place there are some very
important cost factors, above all wages, which in the
nature of the case are not now automatically adjusted to a
general rise or fall in the price level. The advocacy of greater
flexibility has too often in the past boiled down to a one-
sided demand for wage cuts during depressions and thus has
amounted to a defense of other inflexible elements at the
expense of labor. In the third place, there are all the inflexibilities dependent on the fact that long-time contracts,
mortgages, and investments are made in terms of the price
level and the interest rates prevailing at the time of the
transaction and are not revisable with the rise or the fall
of that level. One aspect of this situation is that the fixed
interest obligations on long-term government securities
have assumed a vast importance in view of the enormous
increase in the indebtedness of governments. Only less rigid
are many types of payment which are not contractual in the
same sense as interest or bonded debt but which are fixed

by statute or custom, such as disbursements under unemployment insurance systems, public health services, pension schemes, and the like. Various other rigidities might be cited, such as the salaries of public officials.[1]

To assume that these rigidities will be seriously reduced through any play of laissez-faire forces is to be oblivious to the whole trend of modern civilization. Contractual obligations of all sorts have been increasing in scale and in variety. Social service charges have bulked proportionately larger in the budgets of many European countries than in that of the United States but their extension here must be expected, and if not on economic, then on social and humanitarian grounds, should be welcomed. Wage and salary payments which are not flexible upwards in good times cannot equitably be made flexible downwards in bad times, and in any event the process incurs strong resistances. While the partial price stabilization which exists in such products as steel and aluminum is worse, under recently prevailing conditions at least, than no price stability at all (in that it throws the entire burden of readjustment onto the area of uncontrolled flexible prices), there is no reasonable prospect that the conditions maintaining it can be removed.

Next we come to the extremely important consideration that many of the rigidities we have mentioned depend on the development of the institutional system of modern industry and of the financial and banking organizations which are associated with it. The extraordinary development of the modern corporation is no passing phenomenon but is deeply rooted in the conditions created by modern technique in production and distribution, the rapid advance of facilities of communication, the increase of population, and the consequently greater size of the market for most commodities.

To-day competition in markets dominated by a few great enterprises

[1]See Special Report IV, by Dr. Gayer.

has come to be more often either cutthroat and destructive or so inactive as to make monopoly or duopoly conditions prevail. Competition between a small number of units each involving an organization so complex that costs have become indeterminate does not satisfy the conditions assumed by earlier economists, nor does it appear likely to be as effective a regulator of industry and profits as they had assumed.[2]

In the international area the same tendencies have been operative. On the one hand there is the control of basic products or raw materials through international cartels, pools, valorization schemes, and the like. On the other there are the varied and increasing restrictions placed upon the free international flow of goods. It should be pointed out that the recent heightening of tariffs and other trade barriers has been in part resorted to as a protection against the free play of economic forces impinging from without under the traditional gold standard, when so many rigidities and interferences of various kinds, both within and between countries, have prevented the equilibrium which would justify the unimpeded operation of those forces and made them instead the occasion of new maladjustments.

If we review all these factors of rigidities and frankly recognize their character and extent, the nature of the demand for flexibility, and the very inconsistency of this demand with the laissez-faire premises on which it is based, should become clear. If increased flexibility is to be understood as meaning increased general flexibility it should imply during periods of severe price decline a drastic writing down of capital liabilities unimpeded by any government interference designed to mitigate this ruthless but rapid process of liquidation through wholesale bankruptcy and foreclosure. Rather on these principles should the government, if it intervenes at all, do so for the purpose of encouraging and expediting the process: elasticity in the economic system should imply at such times a deflation not only of wages but also of capital structures even if this involves the

[2]A. A. Berle and G. F. Means, *The Modern Corporation and Private Property*, p. 351.

widespread collapse of big businesses, railroads, insurance companies, and savings banks, regardless of social consequences.

We wish to emphasize, however, that under a policy of internal stabilization whose objective was the preservation of a moving equilibrium in the cost-price structure, a greater flexibility of individual prices and costs would be highly desirable. The aim should be the prevention of instability in the system as a whole but at the same time the promotion of more flexibility within that stable framework. Proposals to this end are made elsewhere in this report. It is, however, a delusion and an anachronism to suppose that sole reliance can be placed on automatic forces. Unless we establish a measure of price stability we are subject to all the disadvantages of the automatic forces in a situation where we cannot reap their reward of equilibrium. To achieve, and to build on the foundation of, this controlled equilibrium (seeing that a "natural" one is precluded by the facts) it is necessary to regulate those institutional systems which are one of the chief factors in the maintenance of rigidities but which, also, unless controlled to this end, would prejudice the objectives which otherwise can be attained under a policy of economic equilibrium.

## 15. *Controls Necessary to Assure the Benefits of Economic Equilibrium*

Various social benefits will accrue directly from the establishment of a system in which prices and costs no longer fluctuate violently and out of relation to one another. The savings of the community will no longer be subject to incalculable fluctuations because they are reckoned by a spurious standard. New savings entrusted to the banking system would continue to represent more nearly the amount of purchasing power the savers handed over. There will not be the involuntary saving which accompanies a drastic price rise or the loss of real saving occasioned by its fall. The activity of industry will not be disturbed as now by the dangerous fever of the speculative inflation of general prices or depressed by the ensuing deflation. Greater assurance will be instilled into valid economic enterprise of every kind. Contracts will be far more secure as well as far more equitably fulfilled, and there will not be the spoliation of creditor and debtor in turn which inevitably accompanies the sharp rise and fall of the price level.

But fully to secure the social benefits of a controlled price level, to make it an adequate means for the regularization of employment and for the utilization of technological advance, to prevent its exploitation also by strong corporate interests, other controls are essential. A reasonably stable price-cost structure should be viewed as a component part of a large measure of public control which will distinguish the freedom of genuine enterprise from the freedom of oppressive power. With such a structure it will be particularly necessary to regulate all organizations which have the power to control either prices or the supply of capital or credit.

Under any price system, no matter how stable, the prices of particular commodities or services are still of course variable. Technological advance is more rapid and more fruitful in some areas of production than in others, and the vicissitudes of supply and demand are still operative. These unequal changes would under competitive conditions be reflected in individual price changes varying in some accord with the variations of cost factors, even though the general price level remained relatively steady. Under monopolistic or quasi-monopolistic conditions the unit-cost reductions are not correspondingly reflected in lower prices. In fact the level of prices might conceivably remain constant because of a rise of monopolistic prices offsetting the fall of competitive prices. This condition would tend to negate one of the large potential benefits of stabilization. The gain due to technological advance is cornered by the controlling interests instead of being shared with the community. If a group of producers can by concerted action or monopolistic control raise the price of their product, they are, in effect, under a stabilized system, compelling other producers and especially the weaker producers, to lower theirs, perhaps by lowering the wages of labor. The argument, therefore, for the control of non-competitive prices is even stronger where a stable price system prevails.

An important aid to such control would be available if all economic corporations, or at least those which float securities publicly and those which have more than a minimum number of stockholders (say one hundred), were obliged to take out Federal charters of incorporation. Constitutional amendment might be necessary to effect this reform. In any event such corporations should be required to follow a standardized method of accounting and to make adequate public statements of their financial position both annually and when any new public financing is being undertaken. There is also a strong case for limiting by law the amount which corporations can borrow, so that their total loans, inclusive of all funds obtained by issuing securities not carrying voting rights, should not exceed, say, the total sum of paid-up subscriptions to full voting stock. Regulation along these lines would prevent much of the excessive investment already discussed and also much of the manipulation for the benefit of insiders which has been so prevalent. That it need not hamper legitimate corporation growth the record of such concerns as American Telephone and Telegraph, General Electric, and other large corporations provides a sufficient testimony.

What applies to corporate control of industry applies no less to banking control. Here in fact regulation should go much further. The private profit-making interests of banks must be made subordinate to the public interest of a balanced economy. To this end the banking system of the country should be unified with respect to policy, this policy being a public and not a private function, while all possible autonomy of administration should be left to the local units. In this process of reconstruction, safeguards should be set up against abuses in the control of investment and other serious defects which have been revealed in the present banking structure. Deposit-creating institutions should be run primarily in the public interest, and to that end the Federal government should supervise the internal administration of the commercial banks. They should be permitted to grant loans only on the basis of financial merit. The government should prevent their manipulation by individuals or groups who, as officers or directors, are interested in giving special preferences to enterprises with which they are associated. Such preferences are contrary to sound social policy, and frequently result in the grant of loans on assets less good than those which other would-be borrowers could offer. It should be made impossible to run institutions which accept and create deposits for the general public as adjuncts to particular businesses or financial enterprises which are operated primarily for the profit of a special inside group. Bank holding companies should be prohibited, unless within very narrow and carefully prescribed limits; and there should be an entire separation of the commercial bank, with respect to organization and personnel, from investment houses, trading syndicates, holding companies, and other financial and industrial corporations.

The commercial banking system of the country should also be unified with respect to legal organization and the application of control. To make this unification effective, the whole commercial banking system of the country should be integrated within the Federal Reserve System. The present absurd arrangement, by which the National Banking and Federal Reserve systems are superimposed upon forty-eight different state systems, does and must stultify all attempts at intelligent, broad control, and renders attainment of the banking aspect of that moving general equilibrium which has been discussed in earlier sections difficult or even impossible. Constitutional amendment may be required to effect this reform, too, but that it is imperative seems clear. Moreover, not only should the power to grant *bona-fide* commercial loans be supervised in the manner suggested in the preceding paragraph, but in addition the power of the commercial banks to make loans and investments for what are in effect long-term capital purposes should be carefully circumscribed, and presumably limited to proportions far lower than those now prevailing. It has become evident that some of the very worst features of the present banking and general financial situation have arisen from the unrestrained and ill-advised financing of long-term capital requirements through the granting of commercial bank loans. The power to create additional bank deposits is one of the most dangerous powers in economic society. It imperatively requires control, and protection against abuse.

Finally, the guarantee of bank deposits, if it continues to be held desirable, should be predicated only on the basis of such a real and adequate supervision of commercial bank assets and operations by the Federal government or its instrumentalities, and of such control as have just been outlined. Without this supervision and control, any system of guarantee which imposes obligations on the solvent banks is manifestly unfair to the better and stronger institutions.

The precise manner in which these goals are best attained is a problem involving much judgment and experience. We cannot deal with it within these limits. There are many difficulties to be met and there are strong interests which will oppose any program directed to these ends. It must suffice to state our conviction that given a realization of the need the country can find the way to overcome it.

### 16. *International Aspects*

In the course of our argument it has been pointed out that there is a close interdependence, in respect of cause and effect, between the breakdown of the gold standard and the increasing restrictions on international trade and the international movement of capital. It is also clear that no satisfactory international monetary system, whether based on gold or not, can be attained unless quota restrictions and the other drastic impediments to international trade are mitigated; while it is no less clear that without the establishment of such a system one of the main incentives to increasing trade barriers will remain in full operation. In short, the restoration of international trade and the development of a genuine international monetary system must be parts of the same program and must be achieved together if they are to be achieved at all. The vicious circle can be broken only by a simultaneous concerted attack on both objectives. And without internal stabilization in the leading industrial countries, and under present conditions most of all in the United States, there is no sure foundation on which progress in either of these directions can be made. Here, as in other relations, internal equilibrium, the assurance of a sound and progressive national order, is the prerequisite of international order.

Consequently we find no essential or permanent opposition between the goal of a more controlled or planned internal economy and the goal of a more controlled or planned international economy. In the last resort it is the operation of the same forces which makes both desirable and necessary. There are in fact at the present time three international requirements the attainment of which would redound alike to our advantage and to the advantage of the whole world: (1) the raising of the world level of whole-sale prices to levels the general criteria of which have already been suggested, followed by serious and systematic endeavors to maintain some kind of stability; (2) the relaxation of trade barriers throughout the world; (3) the reconstruction of a world monetary system to support the higher price level and to give the stability and assurance necessary for the reëstablishment of world trade.

That even during a depression the *reciprocal* reduction of trade barriers would have a beneficial effect we regard as reasonably sure. It would lead, in the countries entering into the agreement, to an increase in real income and would be likely to lead to an increase in the proportion of the national productive resources actively employed. The following are in brief the considerations on which this statement is based:

(1) Assuming that the concessions are fairly evenly balanced, imports will not increase more rapidly than exports, there will not be any net diversion from one country to another of spendable funds, and there will not therefore be in any of the countries any direct impairment of the volume of employment. On the average for all countries this is necessarily true, unless even reciprocal tariff reductions lead to a lowering of the general state of business confidence, which there seems no adequate reason to anticipate.

(2) The lightening of the economic burden of international payments in gold currencies will improve the prospects and the credit status of debtor areas, and this will be a net gain in the general situation and will tend to restore confidence.

(3) In so far as industry has been geared to a given volume of foreign trade and has not been able to shift to production for domestic markets, business funds have been

driven out of existence or into idleness by the multiplication of trade barriers. These funds may come into being or into use again, without corresponding reductions in the use of business funds to serve domestic markets. In this way, general tariff reduction may contribute to business recovery.

The need to safeguard the processes of economic rehabilitation in accordance with the experiments being made under the Industrial Recovery and the Agricultural Adjustment Acts might limit for the present the extent to which the United States can enter into reciprocal trade agreements, but it would certainly not make such arrangements impossible. In this regard also it must be borne in mind that behind all the recent successful protectionist drives for greater national self-sufficiency there has been the profounder and more justified impulsion due to the peril to national programs, social and economic, arising from the unbalanced working of the old international gold standard. Were this peril removed the greatest obstacle to reciprocal trade agreements would also be removed.

How can a workable and generally satisfactory international monetary system be attained? We have already pointed out the conditions on which alone the United States should contemplate a return to gold. If a sufficient degree of international coöperation can be secured among central banks to ensure these conditions, chief among which is that the gold standard will be so managed in future as to secure a reasonable stability, then a return to this much modified and improved gold standard would probably be advisable.[3]

Though the world will perhaps not be ready for the establishment of a genuine international central bank till there comes into being something approaching a world state or world-wide federation of states, yet much might be

[3]See also Special Report VII, by Dr. Gayer.

done to stabilize the value of gold, provided governments and central banks can be persuaded to show the necessary degree of coöperation, by means of an enlargement of the powers and functions of the Bank for International Settlements.

In any reconstruction of a world monetary system, on whatever basis, the services which the Bank for International Settlements could render might well be of very great importance. It is the only established agency through which the central bank authorities of various countries can effectively act in concert. It has peculiar opportunities of situation, experience, and personnel for the handling of the difficult negotiations required for international monetary agreements. It is at present limited, however, by the fact that it can operate only in currencies based on gold. If this limitation were removed, and if its basis of representation were broadened—particularly if the Federal Reserve System were directly represented on its board—it might play a leading rôle in the imminent task of world economic reorganization.

# V. SUMMARY OF CONCLUSIONS AND RECOMMENDATIONS

The transition from a scarcity to a plenty economy which modern technological development is effecting raises profoundly important questions for our times. One is that of the adjustment of economic organization, particularly the money and credit structure, to the productive mechanism in such a way that the potential benefits of technological advance may be most fully actualized and translated into a higher standard of living for the people as a whole. Another is that of the prevention of the grave and increasing fluctuations of economic activity which have thus far accompanied that advance. To these two questions our investigation has been particularly addressed.

Two different approaches are possible in the investigation of these questions. One is economic, the other technological. The former considers the hindrances to potential productivity which lie in economic maladjustments. The latter considers the defects of equipment, skill, application of energy, and coördination of service which interfere with the quantity and quality of output. It is to the former problem that we have addressed ourselves in this report, and in the main only to those aspects of it which are revealed in the great fluctuations of productivity which affect practically all industries at the same time. Thus we deal only with a part of the issue set forth in the introductory sections. It is, however, a part which has peculiar significance at the present time, and it is also the part which seemed most within the competence of the majority of us to examine.

Issues are here involved of such complexity that any conclusions regarding them remain matters of judgment on which differences of opinion and of emphasis are inevitable.

Economic science does not answer our questions but only supplies considerations which may help to guide our judgment. With this proviso the main conclusions of those who sign this report may be summed up as follows.

### 17. *General Conclusions*

(1) We find considerable evidence pointing to a relative failure, even in times reputed prosperous, to make the most effective and economical use of the capacity for production which modern inventions, resources, and powers place at our disposal.

(2) The occurrence of severe fluctuations in business activity is not only in itself one main source of waste and loss of productive power but is a condition which stands in the way of plans for the reduction of other causes of economic waste.

(3) The mitigation of these fluctuations requires the establishment of a balance among the economic factors which, unless controlled, are apt to get out of adjustment and thus induce grave disturbances of business activity. Some factors are subject to sharp fluctuations, others are unduly rigid. Economic equilibrium requires greater stability in the former and greater flexibility in the latter. To this end automatic forces can no longer be exclusively relied upon; for the distinctive differences between highly rigid and highly flexible elements is itself a result of processes in a system of laissez faire.

(4) In particular, the view that the gold standard operated as an automatic regulator of prices must be considerably qualified. In principle, this standard works automatically; in practice, it has been subject, especially in more recent times, to increasing controls exercised through central banks and other agencies. There is thus no longer a clear-cut distinction between a gold-standard currency and a managed currency.

(5) The main reason for this "management" under the gold standard, explaining also why in the last resort so many countries have abandoned or been forced off it, is the fact that under recent and especially post-War conditions the free international movement of gold demanded by the gold standard proved incompatible with the desire of each country to control or regulate its price level and credit policy in terms of its own domestic requirements. In particular, any country which sought to arrest by monetary policies a deflationary trend was either gravely restricted by the danger of international gold movements against it or, if it persisted, was forced off gold altogether.

(6) The need for a reformed monetary system is emphasized by these recent experiences. Such reform is needed both to aid recovery from the depression and as a basis for the solution of the two great problems we have before us. We distinguish therefore between the immediate and the permanent conditions of a satisfactory monetary system.

(7) As for immediate needs, we regard a rise both of domestic prices and of world prices as highly desirable, as a prerequisite to the establishment of a more stable economic equilibrium. So far as the United States at least is concerned, the rise of prices required is one which reflects increased business activity and not one which depends on direct monetary manipulation. For this reason we lay particular stress on the timing of the program of public works.

(8) As for permanent needs, we are impressed with the requirement of a better and more stable balance among a variety of economic factors—between costs and prices, debts and income, saving and investment, and so forth. The achievement of this end is a complicated task for which controls must be progressively worked out in the light of experience and research. Various proposals are made on the subject in the body of the report. One obvious step is to prevent the sharp short-run fluctuations of the price level,

the evil effects of which, both on production and on the distribution of wealth, are enormous. This is an objective quite within reach.

(9) The establishment of economic equilibrium, as already defined, is a necessary condition of any effective national economic planning. We regard economic planning as a rational and in fact a necessary expedient under the conditions of our present society. The contrary doctrine of economic laissez faire assumes a situation of individualist competition and of free price flexibility which, whatever its advantages or disadvantages might be, does not now exist.

On these premises we put forward the following specific recommendations.

## 18. *Specific Recommendations*

(1) In the administration of the recovery program special care should be taken to ensure that the code-making facilities of the National Recovery Act shall not be made a means for the competitive limitation of output by organized industries.

(2) The return of the United States to an international gold standard should be conditional on the assurance of a number of important reforms in the working of that standard, including an agreement by central banks to maintain a reasonable stability of gold itself.

(3) Monetary stabilization should be sought without delay. There are two feasible alternatives in this regard. One is to devaluate the dollar around its present foreign exchange gold value, but at the same time to employ whatever means are expedient to prevent disturbances of the new equilibrium through the repercussions of international gold movements. The other is to maintain the dollar at a reasonably steady rate in terms of foreign currencies, avoiding the attempt to raise prices by inflationary manipulation of its value, but without fixing its gold value until there is assur-

ance that a reformed international gold standard can be set up and maintained. The second alternative has the advantage, provided it is not menaced by political movements, of enabling us to avoid commitment to a permanent standard until the conditions of permanence are guaranteed.

(4) Measures should be taken to maintain an equilibrium in the cost-price structure and in particular to maintain a moving balance between saving, consumption, and capital expansion. Proposals in this direction are contained in the text of the report.

(5) Such measures should include the working out of a national plan for the increase of average wage rates in proportion to the cost reductions attained through technological advance or other means. This is not only equitable in itself but would be an effective means of preventing windfall profits and thereby of securing a more steady flow of money incomes as productive capacity increases. The existing machinery devised under the National Recovery Act could be utilized for this purpose.

(6) We recommend that public works programs should, as a permanent policy, be planned and budgeted sufficiently far in advance to allow them to be conducted on a flexible schedule, being alternately expanded and contracted, in accordance with the needs of the business situation and thus serving as a stabilizing influence. This is necessary in order that monetary measures of credit relaxation or restriction designed to correct symptoms of incipient maladjustments may be reinforced and promptly made effective.

(7) A further step recommended is the establishment of a system of unemployment reserves, or more broadly consumers' reserves, to accumulate in prosperous times and to be drawn upon at the same time that public works programs are accelerated: viz., when symptoms of growing unemployment or slackening business activity appear.

(8) To secure the advantages of economic equilibrium it is particularly necessary to regulate large-scale corporations and such organizations as exert any degree of monopolistic control over prices. This regulation should be directed not only to the price-fixing policies of such organizations but also to their methods of financing, accumulating, and investing reserves, and to the various questions of public interest that arise out of the growth of the modern corporation and the consequent separation of ownership and control. Some suggestions to this end are embodied in the report.

(9) It is no less necessary to regulate all organizations which are concerned with the supply of capital and credit or with the business of investment. Investment houses and commercial banks should be entirely separated. The banking system should be unified and made subject to definite Federal supervision. Federal incorporation, involving membership in the Federal Reserve System, should be obligatory on all banks of deposit.

(10) Internationally, the primary requirements are the raising of world prices, the reduction of trade barriers, and the reconstruction of a world monetary system. There is no essential opposition between these requirements and the requirements of national policy; on the contrary, the achievement of the former would be advantageous to ourselves no less than to the world in general. The prevalent ideal of economic nationalism should certainly not be regarded as implied in the principle of a planned national economy. We recommend therefore that, with due regard to the maintenance of standards established under the National Recovery and Agricultural Adjustments Acts, the United States should pursue agreements for reciprocal tariff reductions.

(11) We recommend that as soon as feasible, and subject to prices being raised sufficiently internally, the United

States should go on record as ready to coöperate with the leading nations in a plan for the reconstruction and maintenance of an international monetary standard.

(12) Finally, we recommend that a National Social-Economic Council, of a purely advisory nature, should be set up and equipped with adequate facilities for research, for the purpose of continuous and concentrated investigation of the main problems of economic planning and with the duty of recommending to the President and Congress such measures as in its judgment would contribute to the balanced economic development of the country.

*(Signed)*

| | |
|---|---|
| ROBERT M. MacIVER | ALVIN H. HANSEN |
| JAMES W. ANGELL | ALVIN JOHNSON |
| JOSEPH W. BARKER | WESLEY C. MITCHELL |
| JOHN M. CLARK | HARLOW S. PERSON |
| ARTHUR D. GAYER | GEORGE SOULE |

JOSEF SCHUMPETER

In signing this report certain members of the Commission wish to append individual statements or reservations on specific points raised in it. These statements follow.

# VI. SUPPLEMENTARY STATEMENTS AND RESERVATIONS OF INDIVIDUAL MEMBERS

## Statement by James W. Angell

I concur heartily in the general tenor and conclusions of the report, but wish to enter reservations on three points of detail in its recommendations.

(1) In Part III, Section 10, and elsewhere, the report advocates that the United States return to the gold standard only under certain conditions, among them monetary and banking agreements with other leading countries. With this erection of conditions I disagree. I believe that a definite return to the full international gold standard at a fixed invariable rate at the earliest possible moment, without regard to the action of other nations, is the wisest step for the United States to take. Uncertainty about the monetary standard is now the chief obstacle to the initiation of substantial business recovery on a wide scale; this obstacle can be removed easily and without danger. The return to gold should presumably be made at a rate corresponding to current foreign exchange quotations, subject to the 50-60 cent limitations imposed by existing and pending legislative acts.

(2) Of the two main alternative objectives with respect to price movements set up in Part III, Section 11, I think the objective of a price level which shall fall with improvements in methods of production is preferable to the objective adopted in the report. I have briefly presented my views on this question elsewhere. Serious practical obstacles stand in the way of the successful execution of either policy. The policy of a gradually falling price level seems to me, however, far easier to enforce from the point of view of the money and banking mechanism; more likely to in-

sure justice as between debtors and creditors; and no more exposed than the alternative policy to the danger that producers will impound the money benefits of technical progress instead of passing them on to the consumers and the recipients of wages and salaries.

(3) I am heartily in sympathy with the objective at which the proposal for establishing consumers' reserves, made in Part III, Section 12, is aimed. I entertain grave doubts of its practicability, however, under our present type of banking system. As things now stand, the accumulation of such reserves would first be likely to induce further expansion of the banking system; and then, when subsequent impending business depression gave the signal for drawing on the reserves, it is likely that the banking system would be unable to meet the drain, because of the severe pressure of liquidation to which it was then being subjected from business at large. The only solution here is such a recasting of the present banking system and practices as would make a genuine impounding and isolation of funds within the system possible.

(*Signed*) James W. Angell

## Statement by Joseph W. Barker

I am heartily in accord with that part of the report of the Columbia Commission on Economic Reconstruction dealing with Productive Capacity and the Economic System.

While the statistical evidence secured by the questionnaire of the subcommittee is limited in number of replies, yet the preponderance of opinion there found agrees in its entirety with published statistical evidence of like character as determined by numerous independent investigations. There can be little or no doubt as to the potential productive capacity of our industries or as to the possible impact of such unrestricted productivity on any economic system of the near future.

With respect to the strictly economic portion of the report, while I am impressed by the validity of the arguments marshalled for "managed currency," I am yet unconvinced that such drastic measures are either immediately necessary or permanently desirable. When economists as eminent as those of our committee cannot agree, an engineer hesitates to express opinions not based on factual study. My general views on the subject of economic controls are represented in the following passages from an article I contributed recently to the *Independent Journal of Columbia University:*

While during the recovery period we may tolerate or even desire general government control of all industry as a purely surgical procedure, it is basic to American ideals that stabilization must concern itself with maintaining the social health of the nation and its people. Yet it must do so with the minimum governmental interference with individual initiative. To secure this minimum we must study our industrial situation searching out those focal points where, if stabilization is secured, the effects automatically spread to the whole system. As possible examples we may consider six—the energy-containing minerals, coal and petroleum agriculture; the basic construction materials, steel, copper, and textiles.

The production of the first two, coal and petroleum, together with relatively stable water-power, govern our fluctuating power supply upon which such a large proportion of industrial civilization depends. Upon the production of the third, agriculture, depends the food supply of our people; and yet here is admittedly the most difficult problem because of the intense individualism of our farmers. Control of the basic construction materials, steel, copper and textiles would automatically govern the production of a very large proportion of the remaining industries and occupations.

It is entirely conceivable that study might show that reasonably generalized stabilization could be secured with control of less than these six focal points, and it is just as conceivable that more than these six or even a different six might be the proper ones. The only point germane to this reasoning is the concept that we should approach stabilization from the point of view of careful study and that control, regulation, or whatever it may be called should be limited to the minimum number of carefully selected focal points. The social health of the nation demands that some form of governor be applied to the industrial machine but, just as in a power station, over-regulation of the machinery is as bad as under-regulation.

There seems to be one other lesson in connection with this regulation of the focal points of control which we can draw from engineering experience in our modern power plants. The more completely automatic the governing action can be made, the better is the final result. Just how such automaticity can be obtained is not at all clear, but is held out only as an objective toward which plans should be drawn or studies conducted.

As an example of the reason for choosing steel as one of the focal points of control it is only necessary to note that the back-log of unfilled orders of the U. S. Steel Corporation has for many years been used as an index of the general condition of business activity. In other words the product of our steel mills is so basic to manufacturing of all kinds that control of the rate of steel production would affect the rate of general manufacturing and construction production. Here we approach the situation where conscious control of the rate of production and the price of the basic material by some form of regulatory body on which government, industry, and labor might be represented would exert a tremendous control over a whole range of industries of all classifications. Steel also answers another highly desirable although not absolutely necessary criterion of a focal point of control, and that is storage of product without rapid deterioration.

It then becomes evident that the plans in use or under discussion to-day are merely recovery plans and have little to do with stabilization. In connection with such plans it is only important that they be considered in two lights—one, do they lead to recovery, and second, do they lend themselves to gradual conversion into a stabilization plan? The wave of criticism of the N. R. A. indicates that the people are restless under the bureaucratic multiplicity of codes and regulations. The Swope plan is a small, tentative step away from bureaucracy, but unfortunately it was announced at a time when the confidence of the people in the integrity of big business has been rocked by the disclosures of the Senate Committee. Just as we do not condemn all government as a result of Tammany graft, neither should we condemn all business as a result of a few unfaithful trustees of business leadership.

I still adhere to the points made in that article, and cannot, therefore, subscribe to that part of the report dealing with currency reforms; but with the general tenor and and conclusions of the report I am in agreement.

(*Signed*) Joseph W. Barker

### Statement by J. M. Clark

I wish to append the following reservation regarding the last paragraph of Part IV, Section 13 (The Meaning of Social-Economic Planning):

As to the effect of national planning on the scope for individual managerial initiative, it does not seem safe to assume that the effect of introducing such planning into the present system, which has no central industrial authority of a comprehensive sort, would be the same as the effect on departmental executives of introducing scientific planning in a business which already has a centralized management of the older type. Nevertheless wise national planning would not necessarily diminish the real scope of managerial initiative. The formal "freedom" of business enterprise at present is a euphemism covering environmental controls, mainly those of the market. In part these impel or coerce management to increase the economy and efficiency of production; in part they lead to courses of action bringing on economic disturbances which prevent the full use of the economy and efficiency which management has developed. The goal of national planning is to substitute at strategic points other forms of environmental control which may (1) prevent or control the forms of action leading to economic disturbance, (2) preserve those leading to economy and efficiency, and (3) leave management freer than it now is to use the economy and efficiency which have been achieved to increase output for the benefit of consumers, and to work out programs of progressive development for the future with greater confidence that the conditions on which they rest will not be swept away. If moderate restrictions on formal liberty could bring freedom from the compulsions of a shrinking market, the result would be a net gain in the substance of liberty.

(*Signed*) J. M. CLARK

## Statement by Wesley C. Mitchell

The preceding report states more effectively than any other document known to me what I take to be the basic economic problem that now confronts mankind—the problem of developing an economic organization that will enable the citizens of a modern state to buy from one another what modern industrial methods enable them to produce. That is a problem with which not only economics but also the other sciences that deal with human behavior may be wrestling for generations to come. As engineering technique has reached its high state of efficiency through the cumulative successes of thousands of men working for generations in many countries, so we must expect that the development of an efficient economic technique will require a long series of discoveries, inventions, and practical trials. No committee working for a single year can solve the problems laid before the present group. But if progress is to be achieved, men who have had the privilege of studying the social sciences must be ready at any time to contribute what in them lies to the age-long process of bettering economic organization by taking thought, however little chance they have of being right at all points.

With the constructive spirit of this report I feel in full accord. Realizing keenly the fallibility of any opinions I can form regarding the best ways of dealing with the intricate problems discussed, I attach no great importance to my doubts concerning certain of the views expressed. Believing that the opinions of my colleagues on the committee are similarly fallible, I commend heartily those passages in the report that stress the need of more penetrating studies of social processes.

(*Signed*) WESLEY C. MITCHELL

## Statement by Harlow S. Person

My agreement with the tenor of this report is so hearty that I do not desire to specify the few particular points in the body of the report with which I do not agree. However, I should like to record my regret that the report does not develop more fully the following concepts: that price adjustments at a price level are more important than a particular price level, and that the increase of social income and not increase of prices is the main issue; that control of credit for investment purposes is of major importance; and that the social control of economic factors indicated throughout the report requires an effective organization for social-economic planning.

(*Signed*) HARLOW S. PERSON

## Statement by George Soule

While I am in general agreement with nearly all of the report, there are two important points on which I ought to record supplementary opinions:

(1) Immediate price policy.—The important objective is not to raise prices but to increase real incomes. The debt burden, for instance, is out of balance, not with prices in the abstract, but with the incomes of debtors. This objective requires (a) raising the prices of commodities which have suffered drastic decline in price but little or no decline in volume of output—e.g., wheat and cotton; (b) increasing the output and sales of goods which have suffered drastic decline in volume but relatively little decline in price— e.g., steel and many manufactured articles. This end may be facilitated by declines in prices of the goods in question. What these varying price movements would do to "the price level" I am uncertain—it would depend on the kind of index consulted. The report is correct in stating that the only desirable increase in prices would be that which might accompany increased economic activity. We ought to be

satisfied with the increased activity if "prices" did not rise. Even in the emergency period, we are really more concerned with interrelationships among classes of prices and among prices and costs and incomes than with any average "price level," for it is these interrelationships which condition the possibility of continued revival when the pump is primed by public works or otherwise.

(2) Permanent control under planning.—The report advocates a high degree of public control over prices, profits, wages, investment of new capital, and the like, in a number of important fields of activity. While it does not attempt to say what form this control would take, the reader is left to infer that it would largely be regulation of privately owned industries. I think the control to be necessary, but believe that so fundamental a control must be exercised administratively rather than by the clumsy methods of regulation. If the public sets the objectives of industry and takes over most of the important major decisions hitherto made by private owners, does it not in fact take over ownership? Of course, "individual initiative would have a large rôle to play in publicly administered industries—the same rôle it now has in private industry among the many subordinates of those who fix the boundaries of policy.

With regard to the last paragraph of Part II, Section 4, suggesting the need of clarification of the Securities Act, I believe it difficult, if not impossible, to modify the Securities Act without allowing loopholes for the abuse of trust. The solution of the problem would seem ultimately to be in public administrative control of new investment under a planning system.

(Signed) GEORGE SOULE

Statement by Josef A. Schumpeter

Dr. Schumpeter's statement appears on p. 239, below.

# SPECIAL REPORTS

## NOTE

These Special Reports express the views of the individual members of the Commission whose names are attached to them. They are to be taken as representing the views of the signatories of the General Report only in so far as they bear out and illustrate the argument of the text of that report. The author of each Special Report is solely responsible for its contents.

# I. REPORT OF SUBCOMMITTEE ON PRODUCTION CAPACITY

## 1. *Introduction*

*Purpose.* Your subcommittee was appointed to inquire whether engineers generally share the view which has been expressed by several members of their profession, that, given a free hand, technical experts could greatly increase income with existing industrial equipment.

*Nature of Inquiry.* The inquiry was obviously not one which permits accumulation and quantitative analysis of mass data. Procedure has necessarily consisted in securing by interviews and questionnaires the judgments of experienced engineers. These judgments are not of such quantity or nature as to permit intensive statistical analysis.

*Discussion Meeting.* Your subcommittee first invited about a dozen prominent engineers to a dinner meeting for general discussion of the subject. This discussion revealed:

(1) Gratification on the part of these engineer guests that a group of economists were giving attention to the subject, and a cordial willingness to coöperate. (Your subcommittee gratefully acknowledges the helpful coöperation which began at this dinner meeting.)

(2) Agreement of all the engineers present with the substance of statements that American industry has already established the technical and material conditions necessary for a vastly greater production of material goods.

(3) Insistence that these statements, especially when they make such specific assertions as "productivity can be doubled," or "consumers can be flooded with goods," must be taken rationally; that no engineer assumes that productivity could and should be increased along all lines suddenly, simultaneously, and equally; that, however, a

very great over-all increase of productivity can be rapidly achieved by increases of the output of each industry in accordance with a natural increase of the demand for its products as conditioned by the simultaneous application of purchasing power to the products of all other industries.

## 2. *The Alford-Hannum Study*

Mr. L. P. Alford and Mr. J. E. Hannum, prominent officials of the American Society of Mechanical Engineers and guests at the dinner meeting, informed your subcommittee that they had been engaged in studies of production capacity which would soon be published, and offered free access to their data. The following is the summary of a statement prepared by them:

Quantitative values for possible increases in the volume of product output that could be brought about by an improvement in man-hour productivity are available for four major industries in the United States, as the result of a special man-hour study by the United States Bureau of the Census, made for the first time in the 1929 Census of Manufacturers.

Increases in the physical quantity of product output that could be brought about by raising the man-hour productivity (total quantity of product output divided by the total number of operating man-hours worked) of the less efficient plants to the level of the average man-hour productivity of the entire industry, without increasing the number of man-hours worked may be estimated, in terms of percentages, as follows:

Blast Furnace Industry...................................... 19%
Lumber and Timber Products Industry........................ 17%
Machine Tool Industry (monetary value)..................... 15%
Petroleum Refining Industry................................ 24%

Increases in the quantity of product output that could be brought about by raising the man-hour productivity of the less efficient plants to the level of the average man-hour productivity of the most efficient group of plants, without increasing the number of man-hours worked, may be expressed, in terms of percentages, as follows:

Blast Furnace Industry...................................... 55%
Lumber and Timber Products Industry....................... 73%
Machine Tool Industry (monetary value)..................... 81%
Petroleum Refining Industry................................ 97%

### 3. *The Martin Study*

Attention is called also to a study of overcapacity by Robert F. Martin, Senior Economic Analyst of the U. S. Bureau of Foreign and Domestic Commerce, published in the *Bulletin of the Taylor Society*, Vol. XVII, No. 3 (June, 1932), pp. 94-99. This study covers ten branches of the iron and steel industry, ten branches of the textile industry, two branches of the glass industry, and the petroleum refining, Portland cement, pearl button, porcelain ware, wheat flour and furniture industries. The data are too voluminous for reproduction here, but with few exceptions in particular years each industry shows unused capacity in every year of the period 1921-1932; some excess in the most active years and large excess in the less active years.

### 4. *The Questionnaire*

Appendix A is the questionnaire sent to 91 prominent engineers and Appendix B is the essentially identical questionnaire sent to 93 prominent major industrial executives. The number of responses was as follows:

|  | ENGINEERS | EXECUTIVES |
|---|---|---|
| Number to whom questionnaire was sent..... | 91 | 93 |
| Number returning questionnaire............. | 34 | 25 |
| Number of questionnaires returned.......... | 45 | 26 |
| Number acknowledging receipt of questionnaire, a few replying to some questions by letter but not returning questionnaire...... | 6 | 4 |
| Number not replying...................... | 51 | 64 |

The industries represented in the returns are: aeroplane; agricultural machinery; asphalt; automobile; book; business machine; carpet and rug (4); coal (3); confectionery; dental supplies; drug; electrical instrument (2); flour milling; furniture (2); gas engine; glass; haberdashery; handkerchief; hosiery; leather belting; machine tool (2 branches); match, paper, and pulp (3 branches); paper-making machinery; paper products (4 branches); rubber (3 branches); shoes (2); soap; steel (6 branches); stove; surgical instrument; textile (6 branches); wire and cable (2).

The replies to specific questions are indicated below. Elaborate statistical analysis is not practicable for lack of homogeneity. The data are judgments; each questionnaire returned reflects usually a different personal equation and a different industry.

*Question* 1 (*Engineers and Executives*). If assured a ready market for all goods produced could the industry reported exceed the best previous record in man-hour output?

|  | ENGINEERS | | EXECUTIVES | |
|---|---|---|---|---|
|  | NO. | PER CENT. | NO. | PER CENT. |
| Number of replies.................. | 45 | ... | 26 | ... |
| Number replying "Yes"............. | 44 | 97.7 | 26 | 100 |
| Number replying "No"............. | 1 | 2.3 | 0 | 0 |

*Question* 1a (*Engineers and Executives*). What per cent of increase could be effected by the industry reported with existing equipment and management?

|  | ENGINEERS | EXECUTIVES |
|---|---|---|
| Number of replies........................ | 42 | 24 |
| Estimates in percentages |  |  |
| Lowest estimate........................ | 10 | 10 |
| Highest estimate....................... | 300 | 300 |
| Mean estimate.......................... | 49.4 | 44.9 |
| Median estimate........................ | 30 | 30 |
| Modal estimate......................... | 27.2 | 50 |

*Question* 1b (*Engineers and Executives*). What per cent of increase could be effected by the industry reported if equipment and management were brought up to the level of the best current standards?

| | ENGINEERS | EXECUTIVES |
|---|---|---|
| Number of replies............................ | 45 | 23 |
| Estimates in percentages | | |
| Lowest estimate........................... | 15 | 20 |
| Highest estimate.......................... | 400 | 350 |
| Mean estimate............................ | 90.1 | 84. 4 |
| Median estimate.......................... | 75 | 62.5 |
| Modal estimate............................ | 100 | 66 |

*Question* 1bb (*Engineers and Executives*). How long a time would be required to bring the industry up to the level of the best current standards?

| | ENGINEERS | EXECUTIVES |
|---|---|---|
| Number of replies............................ | 39 | 22 |
| Estimates in months | | |
| Lowest estimate........................... | 3 | 3 |
| Highest estimate.......................... | 42 | 60 |
| Mean estimate............................ | 17.3 | 14.6 |
| Median estimate.......................... | 12 | 12 |
| Modal estimate............................ | 12 | 15 |

(Note: Replies to questions 1ba., 1bc., and 1bd., concerned with money values—investment, etc.—were so few and confused as to have no significance beyond that of the omissions and confusion).

*Question* 1c (*Executives only*). What per cent of increase could be effected by the industry reported if equipment and management were brought up to the level potential but unrealized in present mechanical and industrial engineering?

| | EXECUTIVES |
|---|---|
| Number of replies.................................... | 16 |
| Estimates in percentages | |
| Lowest estimate..................................... | 25 |
| Highest estimate.................................... | 1000 |
| Mean estimate...................................... | 163.3 |
| Median estimate.................................... | 80 |
| Modal estimate..................................... | 100 |

*Question* 2 (*Executives*). Would your judgment increase the estimate given above if the plants in your industry were coördinated by some form of industrial self-government?

| | EXECUTIVES | |
| --- | --- | --- |
| | NO. | PER CENT. |
| Number replying | 23 | ... |
| Number replying "Yes" | 13 | 56.5 |
| Number replying "No" | 10 | 43.4 |

*Question* 2 (*Engineers*) [*Question* 3 (*Executives*)]. Would it be possible to increase the total output in all industries simultaneously?

| | ENGINEERS | | EXECUTIVES | |
| --- | --- | --- | --- | --- |
| | NO. | PER CENT. | NO. | PER CENT. |
| Number replying | 40 | ... | 25 | ... |
| Number replying "Yes" | 39 | 97.5 | 18 | 72 |
| Number replying "No" | 1 | 2.5 | 7 | 28 |

*Question* 2a (*Engineers*). How much could the output of all industries be increased with existing equipment and methods?

| | ENGINEERS |
| --- | --- |
| Number of replies | 28 |
| Estimates in percentages | |
| Lowest estimate | .. |
| Highest estimate | 150 |
| Mean estimate | 36.3 |
| Median estimate | 27 |
| Modal estimate | 28 |

*Question* 2b (*Engineers*). How much could the output of all industries be increased with equipment and management brought to the level of best current practice?

| | ENGINEERS |
| --- | --- |
| Number of replies | 27 |
| Estimates in percentages | |
| Lowest estimate | .. |
| Highest estimate | 200 |
| Mean estimate | 77.6 |
| Median estimate | 60 |
| Modal estimate | 100 |

*Question* 3 *(Engineers)* [*Question* 4 *(Executives)*]. What physical and managerial obstacles would limit the output if increases were undertaken in all industries simultaneously?

| | ENGINEERS | | EXECUTIVES | |
|---|---|---|---|---|
| | NO. | PER CENT. | NO. | PER CENT. |
| Number of replies.................. | 33 | ... | 25 | ... |
| Shortage of skilled managers......... | 22 | 66.6 | 16 | 64 |
| Inadequate equipment............... | 14 | 42.4 | 10 | 40 |
| Shortage of workers................ | 8 | 24.2 | 6 | 24 |
| Shortage of raw material........... | 5 | 15.1 | 9 | 36 |
| Difficulties of coördination, control, coöperation..................... | 5 | 15.1 | 5 | 20 |
| Shortage of transportation........... | 4 | 12.1 | ... | ... |
| Economic relocation of industry...... | 2 | 6.6 | ... | ... |
| Shortage of power.................. | 1 | 3.3 | ... | ... |
| Shortage of land................... | 1 | 3.3 | ... | ... |
| Inertia............................ | 1 | 3.3 | ... | ... |
| Shortage of storage space........... | 1 | 3.3 | ... | ... |
| Inability to obtain adequate financing... | ... | ... | 3 | 12 |

*Question* 4a *(Engineers)* [*Question* 5a *(Executives)*]. Under conditions of control over operations which have actually prevailed what *economic* factors have limited the volume of output in recent years of active trade (1923-1929) in *the particular industry* reported?

| | ENGINEERS | | EXECUTIVES | |
|---|---|---|---|---|
| | NO. | PER CENT. | NO. | PER CENT. |
| Number of questionnaires............ | 34 | ... | 24 | ... |
| Lack of effective consumer demand... | 21 | 61.7 | 18 | 75 |
| Lack of control: competition—direct and substitution.................. | 13 | 38.2 | 7 | 29.1 |
| Excess costs of distribution and transportation........................ | 6 | 17.6 | 3 | 12.5 |
| Seasonal and style changes.......... | 5 | 14.7 | 1 | 4.1 |
| Lack of adequate equipment......... | 2 | 5.8 | ... | ... |
| Use of obsolete equipment.......... | 2 | 5.8 | 1 | 4.1 |
| Overexpansion of credit............. | 2 | 5.8 | 1 | 4.1 |
| Management wastes and inefficiencies. | 2 | 5.8 | 2 | 8.3 |

| | ENGINEERS | | EXECUTIVES | |
|---|---|---|---|---|
| | NO. | PER CENT. | NO. | PER CENT. |
| Variation in volume of new investment | 1 | 2.9 | ... | ... |
| Unstable currencies | 1 | 2.9 | ... | ... |
| Excess taxes | 1 | 2.9 | ... | ... |
| Lack of knowledge as to capacity of workmen | 1 | 2.9 | ... | ... |
| Improper methods of compensation | 1 | 2.9 | ... | ... |
| Psychology of workers | ... | | 1 | 4.1 |
| Low ethics | ... | | 1 | 4.1 |
| Economic interference with supply and demand | ... | | 3 | 12.5 |

*Question* 4b (*Engineers*) [*Question* 5b (*Executives*)]. Under conditions of control over operations which have actually prevailed, what *economic* factors have limited the volume of output in recent years of active trade (1923-1929) in *industry at large?*

| | ENGINEERS | | EXECUTIVES | |
|---|---|---|---|---|
| | NO. | PER CENT. | NO. | PER CENT. |
| Number of replies | 31 | ... | 22 | ... |
| Lack of purchasing power | 11 | 35.4 | 13 | 59 |
| Lack of financial control, excess credit, speculation | 7 | 22.5 | 3 | 13.5 |
| Uncontrolled competition, lack of planning | 7 | 22.5 | 7 | 31.3 |
| Maldistribution of income | 5 | 16.1 | 3 | 13.5 |
| Failure to depreciate old equipment and utilize new | 5 | 16.1 | ... | ... |
| Excessive merchandising and costs of distribution | 4 | 12.9 | 1 | 4.5 |
| Managerial wastes | 4 | 12.9 | 1 | 4.5 |
| Uncertainties of technological change | 4 | 12.9 | 1 | 4.5 |
| Excessive transportation costs | 3 | 9.6 | ... | ... |
| Tariffs and instability of currencies | 3 | 9.6 | ... | ... |
| Seasonal and style changes | 2 | 6.4 | 1 | 4.5 |
| Employees' fear of working themselves out of jobs | 2 | 6.4 | 1 | 4.5 |
| Improper methods of compensation | 1 | 3.2 | ... | ... |
| Lack of knowledge of workmen's capacity | 1 | 3.2 | ... | ... |

| | | | | |
|---|---|---|---|---|
| Immobility of labor................. | I | 3.2 | ... | ... |
| Inability to maintain uniform price... | I | 3.2 | ... | ... |
| Excess diversion of income into high taxes supporting parasites......... | I | 3.2 | ... | ... |
| Unbalanced price system, rigidities..... | ... | | 3 | 13.5 |
| Low ethical standards................. | ... | | I | 4.5 |

An analysis of the questionnaires according to classification by producer-goods and consumer-goods industries yields the following:

*Question* 1a. If assured a ready market for all goods produced what per cent of increase could be effected by the industry reported with existing equipment and management?

| | ALL PRODUCER-GOODS | | ALL CONSUMER-GOODS | |
|---|---|---|---|---|
| | ENGINEERS | EXECUTIVES | ENGINEERS | EXECUTIVES |
| Number of industries.... | 15 | 10 | 14 | 13 |
| Estimates in percentages | | | | |
| Lowest estimate...... | 24 | 10 | 0 | 10 |
| Highest estimate...... | 300 | 100 | 150 | 300 |
| Mean estimate........ | 45.8 | 38 | 51.5 | 49.6 |
| Median estimate...... | 27.5 | 40 | 37.5 | 27.5 |
| Modal estimate....... | 15 | 47.5 | 75 | 30 |

*Question* 1b. What per cent of increase could be effected by the industry reported if equipment and management were brought to the level of the best current standards?

| | ALL PRODUCER-GOODS | | ALL CONSUMER-GOODS | |
|---|---|---|---|---|
| | ENGINEERS | EXECUTIVES | ENGINEERS | EXECUTIVES |
| Number of industries.... | 15 | 9 | 14 | 13 |
| Estimates in percentages | | | | |
| Lowest estimate...... | 20 | 20 | 10 | 20 |
| Highest estimate...... | 400 | 300 | 300 | 350 |
| Mean estimate........ | 94.2 | 83.8 | 83.6 | 85 |
| Median estimate...... | 60 | 70 | 77.5 | 60 |
| Modal estimate....... | 72.5 | 70 | 95 | 40 |

*Question* 1bb. How long a time would be required to bring the industry to the level of the best current standards?

|                          | ALL PRODUCER-GOODS | | ALL CONSUMER-GOODS | |
|--------------------------|-----------|------------|-----------|------------|
|                          | ENGINEERS | EXECUTIVES | ENGINEERS | EXECUTIVES |
| Number of industries.... | 15        | 9          | 14        | 13         |
| Estimates in months      |           |            |           |            |
|    Lowest estimate...... | 3 | 3 | 6 | 6 |
|    Highest estimate...... | 42 | 24 | 36 | 60 |
|    Mean estimate........ | 18.4 | 7 | 14.4 | 16.3 |
|    Median estimate...... | 18 | 12 | 12 | 12 |
|    Modal estimate....... | 12 | 10 | 6 | 16 |

## 5. *Suggestions*

Your subcommittee suggests that because the judgments assembled by the questionnaire are essentially unanimous they must be given most serious consideration. The question at issue—whether, assuming an unlimited market, with present capital equipment, labor, and materials, a large increase in the production of material goods is possible—is not one which can be answered directly by experience, because the market has been limited. Yet here is an indirect answer from trained engineers and able executives, experienced with machinery and management. It should not be forgotten that survival in their professions and in their businesses has depended on the development of a capacity for reasonably accurate judgments and estimates— a sixth sense of the same order as that of the timber cruiser who can estimate the feet of standing timber in a forest by walking through it, and on whose judgment large investments are safely made.

If we accept the judgment of these fifty-nine engineers and executives that from the viewpoint of engineering technology the productivity of industry could be greatly increased with existing facilities, were it not for limits to effective demand, interest is turned at once to this matter of effective demand. Experience promptly rejects the hypothesis that demand is restricted because all—or anywhere near all—consumer wants are satisfied. Presumably, therefore, the restriction of demand is caused by ineffectiveness, due to the existence of interfering institutions or the absence of essential institutions, in the functioning of the processes whereby total income is distributed and transformed into purchasing power. Were real income properly, promptly, and smoothly distributed and transformed into purchasing power, productivity and the standard of living could be increased indefinitely through a continuous dynamic interaction and adjustment. It is at this point, your subcommittee suggests, that the inquiry of the Commission should be focused. It suggests more specifically that it be focused on the characteristics of the distribution of the social income, the price system and institutions which affect it, and the matter of balance between industries according to the demands made upon them respectively by consumer choices.

(*Signed*) JOSEPH W. BARKER
WESLEY C. MITCHELL
H. S. PERSON
*Subcommittee*

October 16, 1933

APPENDIX A TO SPECIAL REPORT I
*Questionnaire Sent to Engineers*

President Butler of Columbia University recently appointed a Commission on Economic Change and invited it to make constructive suggestions regarding the existing economic organization.

This Commission has been much interested in the opinion expressed by prominent engineers that, if given a free hand, technical experts could at least double the largest real income attained in any past year by the people of the United States. As an illustration of this view, the following rather journalistic statement by Mr. Ralph E. Flanders, recently Vice-President of the American Society of Mechanical Engineers, may serve:

The engineer knows—all engineers know—that if some omniscient dictator were installed as ruler of the United States, they could provide for him raw material, machinery, and trained labor sufficient to flood, bury and smother the population in such an avalanche of food, clothing, shelter, luxuries, and material refinements as no Utopian dreamer in his busiest slumbers has ever conceived. The material conditions for productivity are already here, but to control the economic machine we need more than the ability, the means, the raw materials with which to produce.

The Commission wishes to learn whether many competent engineers share the view in question. Might the production of real income and services be carried far above the highest levels yet reached if we were able "to control the economic machine"? For this purpose a subcommittee has prepared, with the advice of several engineers, the enclosed questionnaire which it is sending to a brief list of prominent members of the engineering professions.

Most of the questions call for qualitative rather than quantitative answers. *Where estimates are asked for, no more than rough approximations can be expected.* If the sample of opinion obtained sustains the view that the limits upon the production of real income are not of a technical engineering sort, but primarily economic in character, the need for a more searching inquiry will be demonstrated.

Since conditions vary from industry to industry, and since the engineers to whom this letter goes may have expert knowledge of several fields, three copies of the questionnaire are enclosed. Additional copies will be supplied if desired. A separate copy should be filled in and returned for each definitely indicated industry or field.

With deep appreciation for the help you will render the Commission by filling out and returning the attached questionnaire, we are

Yours very truly,

(*Signed*) WESLEY C. MITCHELL

HARLOW S. PERSON

*Subcommittee of the*

*Commission on Economic Reconstruction*

Detach this questionnaire and return it in accompanying addressed and
stamped envelope to H. S. Person, Room 2360,
420 Lexington Avenue
New York, N. Y.

*This reply will be considered confidential*

## ENGINEERING POSSIBILITIES OF
## INCREASING NATIONAL REAL INCOME

Date.....................................

Name...............................................................................................

Address ...........................................................................................

Industry covered by following answers.........................................

Leading product or products........................................................

1. If given full control of operation and assured
   a market for all goods produced, could engineers exceed the best previous records in man-
   hour output of the products named above, or
   in output per machine-hour if the man-hour
   unit is not appropriate to the industry
   named? (Do not consider an increase of
   standard working hours as a means of increasing output.)      Yes.............. No..............

   *How great an increase* could engineers effect in
   the output of this industry as a whole on
   above conditions

   With existing equipment?      ...........................per cent

   With existing equipment brought up to
   level of best current standards?      ...........................per cent

       How large an investment would be re-
       quired for this latter purpose?      $...........................

       How much time would the reconstruc-
       tion work require?      ...........................months

       How much existing investment in plant
       would be scrapped by this change?      $...........................

       Would the investment in new equipment
       per unit of output be greater or less than
       the book value of the equipment dis-
       placed?      Greater...........Less...........

2. If given full control of operation and assured
   a market for all goods produced, could en-

gineers increase total output above best previous records *in all industries at the same time* without increasing standard working hours? Yes.............. No..............

How great an increase above best previous records could engineers effect in output on above conditions

With existing equipment? ............................per cent
With equipment brought up to level of best current standards? ............................per cent

3. If an all-round increase of production were undertaken, what *physical* obstacle would limit volume of output?

Shortage of workers................ Shortage of raw materials................
Shortage of skilled managers.............. Inadequate equipment..............
Other limiting factors (please specify)................................................
................................................................................................
................................................................................................

4. In actual practice, under existing conditions of control over operations, what *economic* factors have limited the volume of output in recent years of active trade (1923-1929)

A. In the industry named above?................................................
................................................................................................
................................................................................................
................................................................................................

B. In industry at large?................................................................
................................................................................................
................................................................................................
................................................................................................

## APPENDIX B TO SPECIAL REPORT I
### Questionnaire Sent to Industrial Executives

President Butler of Columbia University recently appointed a Commission on Economic Change and invited it to make constructive suggestions regarding the existing economic organization.

This Commission has been much interested in the opinion expressed by prominent engineers that, if given a free hand, technical experts could at least double the largest real income attained in any past year by the people of the United States. As an illustration of this view, the following rather journalistic statement by Mr. Ralph E. Flanders, recently Vice-President of the American Society of Mechanical Engineers, may serve:

> The engineer knows—all engineers know—that if some omniscient dictator were installed as ruler of the United States, they could provide for him raw material, machinery, and trained labor sufficient to flood, bury and smother the population in such an avalanche of food, clothing, shelter, luxuries, and material refinements as no Utopian dreamer in his busiest slumbers has ever conceived. The material conditions for productivity are already here, but to control the economic machine we need more than the ability, the means, the raw materials with which to produce.

As a subcommittee of the Commission we have sent to a list of about seventy-five selected engineers a questionnaire intended to ascertain whether they are in substantial agreement with the viewpoint expressed by Mr. Flanders.

However, the questionnaire addressed to them is concerned only with man-hour or machine-hour outputs of mechanical equipments and processes, and not with unused capacity, uneconomical management, duplication of facilities, waste of excessive competition, etc.

We desire also to bring to bear on the problem the judgments of executives of large experience who are asked to consider the matter in broader perspective. Accordingly we are sending this questionnaire to about seventy-five selected industrial executives.

Most of the questions call for qualitative rather than quantitative answers—for intuitive judgments rather than demonstrated conclusions. *Where estimates are asked for, no more than rough approximations can be expected.* In the absence of quantitative data such judgment will be of great value. If the sample of opinion obtained sustains the view that the limits upon the production of real income are not of a technical engineering, managerial, and organization sort, but primarily economic in character, the need for more searching inquiry will be demonstrated.

With deep appreciation for the help you will render the Commission by filling out and returning the attached questionnaire, we are

Yours very truly,

(*Signed*) WESLEY C. MITCHELL

HARLOW S. PERSON

*Subcommittee of the*

*Commission on Economic Reconstruction*

Detach this questionnaire and return it in accompanying addressed and stamped envelope to H. S. PERSON, Room 2360, 420 Lexington Avenue, New York, N. Y.

*This reply will be considered confidential*

## POSSIBILITIES OF INCREASING REAL INCOME

Through Better Organization, Use of Facilities and Management in Industry

Date...................................

Name.........................................................................................................................

Address.....................................................................................................................

Industry covered by answers.................................................................................

Principal product or products...............................................................................

IMPORTANT: Make the following assumptions in answering all questions except No. 5: (1) Neither increase nor decrease in standard working hours; (2) A ready market for *all* goods produced.

1. Considering your own industry only, if the situation were in accordance with the above assumptions, could the industry surpass the best previous records of total output?    Yes........... No................
   a. With existing equipment and management?    ...............................per cent
   b. With existing equipment and management brought up to the level of the best current standards?..................    ...............................per cent
      How large an investment would be required for this latter purpose?    $.............................

How much time would the develop-
ment work require?                                     .............................months

How much existing investment in
plant would be scrapped by the
change?                                               $..........................

Would the investment in new equipment per unit of output be greater or
less than the book value of the in-
vestment displaced?                                   Greater......... Less............

c. With existing equipment and management brought up to the level practically
   potential in present mechanical and industrial engineering, but not yet re-
   alized?                                            .............................. per cent

2. Would your judgment increase the estimates
   given above if the plants in your industry
   were coördinated by some form of industrial
   self-government?                                    Yes............... No...............
   a. Re-estimate of 1. a. above                      ..............................per cent
   b. Re-estimate of 1. b. above                      ..............................per cent
   c. Re-estimate of 1. c. above                      ..............................per cent

3. Taking into consideration not only your own
   but *all* industries, would it in your judgment
   be possible to increase the total output of *all*
   industries simultaneously?                         Yes............... No...............

4. If such simultaneous increase of output in all
   industries were undertaken, what physical
   and managerial obstacle(s) would limit volume of output?
   Shortage of workers ................. Shortage of raw materials................
   Shortage of skilled managers............... Inadequate equipment..............
   Any other limiting factors................................................................
   ........................................................................................
   ........................................................................................

5. Discarding the assumptions which applied to the questions above—
   Under conditions of control over operations which have actually
   prevailed, what *economic* factors have limited the volume of output
   in recent years of active trade (1923-1929)

a. In the industry named above?.................................................................

.................................................................................................................

.................................................................................................................

.................................................................................................................

b. In industry at large?.................................................................................

.................................................................................................................

.................................................................................................................

.................................................................................................................

## II. PRODUCTIVE CAPACITY AND EFFECTIVE DEMAND

BY J. M. CLARK

This report addresses itself in the main to the problems raised by the memorandum of Messrs. Barker, Mitchell, and Person, of productive capacity remaining chronically unutilized, even in good times. However, since one hypothesis as to the reason for this condition attributes it to cyclical fluctuations in industrial activity, that problem also necessarily enters into the discussion. The central problem here taken up is, first, whether there exists a condition which can be correctly described as a chronic limitation of production owing to limitation of effective demand, and second, if it does exist, what is the nature and meaning of the condition which is commonly so described? Underlying this is the analysis of the nature of the mechanism by which potential power to produce is transformed into realized production, balanced and activated by an equivalent effective demand for the products turned out. No definitive analysis of this sort has been made; and all that can be done in a report of this character is to suggest hypotheses bearing upon it, subject to verification by the researches of many economists.

As to the facts, the memorandum of Barker, Mitchell, and Person affords a starting point. It is presented only as a fragmentary sampling of the field; and the sample is probably to some extent a biased one. In manufacturing, one expects to find such conditions as are suggested by this memorandum; while agriculture, housing construction, mining, transportation, mercantile distribution, and various classes of services each have their own peculiar conditions, and the margin of unused productive capacity on the average of all these fields would, beyond reasonable doubt, be smaller than in manufacturing.

The impressions of engineers and executives as to the causes of limited output are also subject to some qualification. In particular, it is quite possible that if the factor which they feel as the present limiting one were to cease to act as a limitation, other limiting factors would come to bear and would limit output long before theoretical capacity was attained. Means of transportation and mercantile distribution might act in this way. But it is also fair to assume that if limitations due to "limited demand" were removed, these other limiting factors would be expanded, at a cost which would dilute the resulting gains but not completely cancel them. The present special report will assume that it has been reasonably well established that there exists a very considerable margin of unused productive capacity owing to the condition commonly thought of and spoken of as limited effective demand.

Another qualification is the moral certainty that if by a miracle there should be brought into existence a volume of effective demand equal to the existing unused productive power, that demand would not be directed to buying just those goods and services for which the economic system has unused capacity, and in precise proportion to the unused capacity existing. Therefore a complement to this study is the study of the standard of living which is attainable, so far as our power to produce is concerned. Only the most uncertain estimates could be made; but even these might be useful.

To indicate the difficult nature of the problem, one might start with a provisional assumption that a general increase of twenty-five per cent is possible, only to find that if increased income were largely concentrated in the hands of a few wealthy groups, so little of the increased demand would go to the mass-production industries where the chief untapped powers of production lie that the increase would be cut to ten per cent, even if an oversaving crisis could somehow be avoided. On the other hand, if the increase were accompanied by a radical equalizing of income, the resulting demand might be so concentrated on the mass-production industries that a twenty-five per cent increase would fall far short of exhausting the possibilities, if the motivation of industry were not impaired. The Chamber of Commerce of the United States has made a survey of the possible increase in demand growing out of a general stand-ard of living of $2,500 per family. Such studies need to be correlated with possible increases in production and think-able systems of distribution of the proceeds.

For instance, in New York the $2,500 family income would still fall just short of affording an effective demand for a modern four-room apartment built on a commercial basis, unless the family spends a larger percentage of its income for rent than is considered good budgeting. At pres-ent there is a wide gap between the highest rent the great mass of the people can pay and the lowest rent at which new commercial construction is practicable. But if incomes were to increase and construction costs to come down, somewhere there would be reached a critical point at which a vast new effective demand would be tapped; and the re-sulting economies of larger-scale building would justify lower prices; and might free the mass of the people from the necessity of living in obsolete and unfit quarters.

Lacking such studies of potential demand and supply, we still know beyond a doubt that our system has actually assimilated great increases in productive power since the beginning of the Industrial Revolution, converting them into actual realized increases in production. This is a basic fact to be placed alongside the proposition that the system has not assimilated its productive power as fast as that power has come into being. And the question "Why has the system not assimilated all its productive power?'' might as well be reversed. Why and how has it assimilated as much as it has? Why should we expect that it would assimilate it all? Why should not considerable groups of laborers, for instance, be pushed outside the circle of production, reward, and power to buy goods and not be able to make their way in again?

It may help us in attempting to analyze the mechanism for assimilating progress to look at some of the adjustments which this mechanism has to make, if it is to do its work successfully. In the first place, one of the things to be assimilated is an ever-increasing supply of capital per worker. This goes into more and more automatic machinery, whereby one worker controls more and more spindles, or more and more working power in other forms, with a correspondingly increased output per worker. If the new capital goes into needless duplication of existing types of plant, then to that extent it is being wasted, and the productive power it contains is not being successfully used. Since this actually happens to a considerable extent, the conclusion is that a full use of our supply of capital would call for a more rapid development of labor-saving equipment than we have actually witnessed, if it is all to be absorbed without useless duplications.

The resulting increase of output cannot take the shape simply of an even expansion in all lines. Foodstuffs cannot increase very much without glutting the market, manufactured goods in general have vastly more elastic possibilities, while services of an intangible sort have the greatest possibilities of all. To absorb the rising standard of living made possible by improvements in steel-making and the textile industries, we may be called on to employ a smaller percentage of our labor force there and a larger percentage in caring for our health and recreation. But it is not precisely those individuals who would be thrown out of work in steel and textiles whom we should want to employ in these much more responsible service capacities. Evidently the shift involved is a highly complex one. It becomes a trifle more simple to the extent that we enlarge our demands for tangible goods. But this requires the continual development of new commodities, which typically begin as luxuries for the well-to-do and finally make their way into quantity production at lowered costs which bring them within the reach of increasing numbers. Another item in the adjustment is a shortening of the hours of labor, whereby the workers get part of the benefit of increased productive power in the shape of leisure, and part in the shape of more goods.

Finally, we have to reckon with a tendency toward saving a progressively increasing proportion of our income as our income itself gets larger. Thus the whole process may need to go faster and faster, if the whole of the increasing productive power is to be utilized. And it is really very little wonder if some parts of this very complicated process do not proceed fast enough or accurately enough. A competent socialist government with the best possible planning board would not be able to avoid all mistakes and misfits. It might easily be reduced to the expedient of cutting down working hours, perhaps from eight to six, in spite of the fact that the workers might prefer to work nine hours if they could get correspondingly more goods.

The main items in the mechanism by which private business takes care of this process seem to be the following: (1) the willingness of business enterprise to produce in anticipation of demand either (*a*) some new commodity or (*b*) new equipment to produce a familiar commodity more economically; (2) an elastic credit system which can furnish business enterprise funds for expansion without waiting for individuals to pile up original savings enough to finance the projects in hand (The savings can come afterward, out of the earnings of the new equipment or the new enterprises, if they are successful. This carries with it a corollary which may not be so fortunate, namely that there is an increase in the volume of our real medium of exchange, all of which goes to finance producers' goods. There are other forms of credit used to finance consumers' goods, but there is no assurance that they expand and contract in such a way as to maintain a healthy balance between consumers' and producers' purchasing power); (3) reduced prices, to dispose of increased amounts of goods turned out at decreased unit costs; (4) decreased wage demands on the part of any workers who have been displaced, as a means of making it worth while for some employer to take them on again; (5) lower interest charges to make it worth while for employers to use capital fairly lavishly in order to economize labor; (6) increased consumer purchasing power resulting from the expenditures which producers have made in expanding production or doing other kinds of pioneering, or the disbursement of the earnings which have come to the successful ones.

Another factor in the situation is the stock market, which intervenes between people who save funds and businesses which put them into buildings, machines, and working capital. The stock market is one of the agencies for expanding production, but its operations too often lead to speculative booms which do not help the sound progress of the whole system.

If the circulating medium remained fixed in quantity, and its circuit velocity unchanged, no increased quantity of goods could find a market except at a proportionately lowered average price level. If some goods find a market in increased volume without corresponding decrease in price, they take up purchasing power formerly going into other goods, with the result that these other goods must sell either at a lower price or in smaller volume. If prices cannot or will not make all these adjustments in the way which permits increased output, then another factor must take up the burden of adjustment. If business cannot endure a falling price level, then the circulating medium or its circuit velocity must increase. Increase in volume of production is limited to the increase in the product of the volume of the circulating medium by its circuit velocity.

Neither the circulating medium nor prices are absolutely rigid; but our system is apparently more and more closely approximating the last condition mentioned: i.e., that of an economy which tolerates no general declines in prices of considerable magnitude, in the sense that it resists them so strongly at many points that they can never be carried through as balanced *general* movements, and never without precipitating a depression. And as the "circuit velocity" of money is largely an independent factor, this amounts to saying that in a general and approximate way, increased output is limited by increase in the circulating medium, modified by a certain tolerance of the system for relatively slow and mild declines in prices.

While these conditions as to volume of the medium of exchange and general price movements are necessary to absorption of potential productive power, they are not alone sufficient. There may be enough purchasing power in the economic system to take anything a given business man may produce with a part of the country's disengaged resources; but that is no guarantee that this purchasing power will actually be used to take off the market whatever this particular business man may see fit to produce. And if it is not used in this way, then the continuous flow of purchasing power which should result from this business man's operations will never come into being.

Purchasing power is not merely volume of circulating medium times its circuit velocity divided by the index of the price level. If this expression be analyzed, it reduces itself to a much simpler one: physical quantity of goods produced. Purchasing power and physical output are two aspects of the same thing, and real purchasing power can be increased only by measures which result in increasing physical output: measures which end by reducing physical output can only reduce real purchasing power and not increase it.

But this does not mean all it may seem to mean on the surface. It does not mean, for example, that all that is needed to increase purchasing power is to produce more of anything, no matter what. Only goods that sell in the market constitute purchasing power for other goods; and only goods that sell for enough to cover the minimum or "variable" or direct costs of production will continue to sell at all. Whenever goods are selling for less than cost, it means that the resources used to produce these goods are not bringing into being as much purchasing power to buy other products as is latent in these resources. But in this statement the assumption is made that the money costs of the productive resources are adjusted at what is supposed to be the normal level. The upshot of the matter is that while output of one salable product constitutes purchasing power for other products, a producer may be bringing into being more or less purchasing power, or in limiting cases none at all, according as he makes something which will sell for more or less than the resources used to produce it could have yielded elsewhere, or something which the market will not take at any price which the seller is willing to accept.

The bearings of this discussion on the question at issue can be summed up by saying that adequate purchasing power is not merely a matter of volume of the circulating medium, or even of the total flow of money incomes, divorced from what happens to prices. The ultimate basis of purchasing power is production itself; and adequate purchasing power depends on the successful making of all the far-reaching adjustments already mentioned as necessary to the assimilation of increased power to produce goods.

The volume of media of exchange can be increased by credit inflation, bringing about an immediate increase in purchasing power not dependent on prior increase of production—and this is an important factor; but apart from a rather moderate long-run upward trend such increases are temporary. If they do not result in an increase in production, so adjusted as to be lasting, they produce only a momentary increase in real purchasing power.

Shifts of income from one group to another may involve momentary increases or decreases in the active flow of purchasing power, if the income is shifted from groups who receive it and use it more promptly to those who receive and use it more slowly, and *vice versa*. Such shifts may also affect the balance of the economic system by altering demand as between different kinds of goods, or altering the relative amounts of consumers' spending and saving. If such shifts have the effect of improving the whole adjustment of the economic system, in terms of all the elements already discussed, they may increase real purchasing power; but not otherwise.

We may now pass on to the question of why potential productive powers are not fully used, and consider those causes whose immediate and visible symptom appears in the form of an inadequate market for the products. Here two hypotheses stand out. The first has to do with long-run trends, and assumes that there is some limitation on the increase of purchasing power, or on the rate at which the economic system can make the adjustments which have been outlined, such that this rate falls short of the rate of increase in our powers of production. The second hypothesis is that good times always start from a depression, and are attained by methods and processes of such a sort that they can go only a limited distance before they come to an end and create a condition bringing on a reaction, without ever reaching the point of full utilization of our powers of production.

Both hypotheses may be true; but if the second is true, it means that industrial fluctuations are the first obstacle to full use of our productive powers, and until they are measurably dealt with, we can hardly test the truth of the first hypothesis, or grapple very usefully with the problems which it raises. The present writer inclines to the view that the second hypothesis is true, with the consequences just pointed out.

The mechanism of expansion from depression to boom may be divided into sources of the original impulse to expansion and sources of its cumulative effects. Leaving out of account the original initiating impulses, which may be of a great variety of sorts, the sources of cumulative expansion center chiefly in the class of durable goods, in which by far the greatest percentage of expansion and contraction is found. This includes capital equipment and durable consumers' goods, among which the dominant items are housing and automobiles. These goods have one common characteristic of vital importance: namely that an upward deflection of, let us say, five per cent in the course of the total supply of capital equipment or of housing space calls for much more than a five per cent increase in the current output of these goods.

If the production of these goods had to wait until people accumulated enough actual income to buy the houses for cash, or enough original personal savings to furnish funds for the capital expansion, these features tending toward intensified fluctuations would have little chance to operate. But such goods are bought on credit, and credit is elastic and makes it possible to buy the goods first and accumulate the income or savings afterwards, with the result that capital equipment can be paid for out of its own ultimate earnings, if these are sufficient. It is often installed without waiting for realized demand for the products.

But the process of installing it creates demand: that is, it brings about a diffusion of spending power among all who share in the income derived from making and installing the equipment; and this is the central fact in the general diffusion of the effects of such an expansion. The revival in the work of making capital equipment is an intensified reflection of the forces that gave rise to it; and it brings about a further revival in demand for things in general. This in turn is reflected back in a still stronger increase in demand for capital equipment; and the movement is further intensified by the speculative effects of rising prices, and by a general feeling of optimism.

Such a self-reinforcing expansion cannot go on forever, if only because it must at some point reach the limits of expansion of the credit system. It reaches the limits of safe expansion even sooner, since the basis of the credit is the earning power of the productive equipment which is being brought into being; and this rests on a shaky foundation. The rapid expansion in the durable goods industries is not an enduring thing, but a concentration, let us say, of two years' growth in one. There must some time come a tapering off in the rate of expansion, and when it comes, the buying power of consumers in general tapers off as a direct result. The further result in these durable goods industries is an absolute decline·in the rate of production needed to satisfy the demand. This means an absolute decline in the amounts distributed as spending power to those who share in the income from these branches of production, and a corresponding decline in the effective demand for things in general. The cumulative effects of the movement are now reversed.

A further fact is that at the peak, people with more income than usual are saving a larger percentage of it than usual, and spending a smaller percentage for consumers' goods. Thus demand for consumers' goods in general does not increase as fast as productive power, so that the tapering-off process which starts the reversal is an inevitable thing. The expansion is bound to find a limit. Another source of instability is the fact that credit is debt, and the elastic type of credit is short-time or callable debt, the expansion of which introduces an explosive element into the situation.

The central facts may be put arithmetically. If an original increase of five per cent in demand for consumers' goods calls forth an increase of thirty per cent in the current output of durable means of production, as is fairly probable, the increased activity in producing capital equipment, spread over the whole field of industry, would amount to something like an additional five per cent increase in total production. If the original impulse were of a temporary sort, and had disappeared by the time the secondary effects came into being, the thing would end there. The thirty per cent expansion in the work of making capital equipment might be maintained until the total amount of productive capacity was adjusted to a five per cent increase in output, but then it would come to an end and a general contraction would result unless something else had in the meantime started another upward impulse of the cumulative sort.

If the original impulse did not vanish as soon as the secondary effects came into being, there would be a ten per cent increase in demand for things in general, which might quite possibly result in a sixty per cent increase in the demand for capital equipment, which in turn would lead to a still further increase in general demand for consumers' goods, and so on until some neutralizing factor appeared, or until the credit system could expand no farther.

If we take the process at the point where the output of

capital equipment has expanded sixty per cent, this may mean possibly only a six per cent increase in productive capacity during the first year, which is less than the expansion in general demand. Thus there is a sellers' market with rising prices, and the other usual accompaniments. But if this condition keeps on, productive capacity will soon increase beyond the increase in general demand which the equipment boom is itself sustaining, by an inherent mathematical necessity.

This condition may be described in terms of failure of purchasing power to keep pace with power to produce, but the discrepancy seems inherent in the concentrated spurt of expansion in productive facilities. It is difficult to see how, in the nature of the case, purchasing power for goods in general can keep pace indefinitely with productive power when the increase of the latter has behind it the whole force, or the main force, of credit expansion. And when the expansion of capital equipment tapers off, general purchasing power declines. Thus the behavior of the production of durable goods seems to lie behind the shortage of purchasing power.

One further fact seems to be that the conditions of a boom in capital equipment act as an obstacle to the making of one of the adjustments which are necessary in the long run to the absorption of increased productive power. A general increase in the supply of capital per worker needs to be put in new forms of an increasingly automatic sort, rather than in mere duplication of plants of the existing types. If this were wisely done, it would reduce costs of production, though the output per thousand dollars of capital would not be as great as before. Then a condition of excess capacity would not come so quickly, and, when it did, the industries would be in a position to meet it by lowering prices and marketing an enlarged output in the face of a limited volume of dollar purchasing power.

But the condition of a capital-equipment boom is hostile to such a development. Expanding productive capacity, rather than reduced cost, is the thing sought, and the urgency is so great that conditions of future efficiency tend to be neglected. A limited supply of labor may still act as an incentive to developing more labor-saving types of equipment, as may also high wages maintained by strong unions in particular industries; but the typical outcome seems to be an undue amount of duplication of facilities of generally familiar types, rather than a change in the type adequate to absorb the full increase in the supply of capital per worker which is coming into being.

Lower interest rates would facilitate the proper adjustment, but in a time of expansion interest rates tend to be increased rather than reduced. They exceed the social productivity of added capital when that capital is being put into wasteful duplication and excess capacity. This condition acts as an obstacle to lower-grade uses of capital which could be made to yield a moderate, but real, social product.

Changing the forms of capital equipment would not solve all the problems of assimilating increased power to produce goods; it would merely be one step in the right direction. In fact, in the long run it would actually speed up the increase in per capita productive power, at the same time that it put industry in a somewhat better position to absorb such increases. It would not solve all the questions of what to produce, how to distribute income, how much to shorten hours of labor, and so forth. The short-run problems of the business cycle would be somewhat mitigated, but not cured, while the long-run problems of absorbing increased productive power would remain.

As to the short-run problems, the natural remedy would surely not be to try to pump enough extra dollar purchasing power into the economic system to take care of all the increase of productive power which a credit boom can finance, and to do it without any reduction in the level of prices. There seems to be no sound way of doing that. The more appropriate remedy would be to regularize the expansion of capital facilities, and so far as possible of durable goods in general, so that it will not go by spurts which cannot in the nature of things be maintained. This is no easy task, but it is vitally necessary, and it would be premature to say that it is impossible. Some suggestions bearing on it are contained in the concluding paragraphs of an article by the present writer, to appear in the March, 1934, number of the *American Economic Review*.[1]

Another appropriate measure, and one which seems necessary and inevitable, is to make the flow of available purchasing power more stable than the flow of productive activity, by the use of stabilizing reserves. Dividend reserves are already common practice, and unemployment reserves would be a logical complement. But there are dangers to be avoided. The financial handling of the reserves, and the methods of realizing on them when benefits are to be paid, may defeat any purpose of stabilizing general purchasing power, and merely result in concentrating the fluctuations on the things in which the reserve funds are invested. Buying securities during booms and making forced sales during recessions will not be wise financing or helpful to the general situation; but other and better methods can be devised.

Another danger is that, if the benefits are too liberal, the result may be to stiffen unduly the wage rates below which workers would rather remain idle than accept employment. This, by reducing the flow of goods, would reduce real purchasing power instead of increasing it. In short, this device of unemployment reserves is a delicate instrument, which may do harm as well as good, and requires careful and

[1]The article will appear under the title: "Economics and the National Recovery Administration."

courageous handling to produce the benefits of which it is capable.

If and when, by these means or others, we make substantial progress toward greater stability, we can face the further problem whether people spend too little for consumption, and save too much, for a balanced supply of capital in the forms into which we know how to convert it; and whether changes in the distribution of income can do something to improve the balance. It is, of course, a desirable thing that real purchasing power should expand as fast as possible. And it seems a primary consideration that it will, over a term of years, expand faster if it does so continuously and without the setbacks that follow our periods of concentrated expansion. On the other hand, this process would actually sharpen some of the problems that face us; particularly that of casual and semi-casual labor. Regularization might mean permanent unemployment for considerable numbers of those who are able to get along under customary conditions with irregular or occasional jobs.

If, under regularization, the natural expansion of means of payment does not go on fast enough to absorb our possible output without reduced prices, the soundest way of expanding real purchasing power, on the whole, is to lower prices. This may or may not be necessary as a long-run tendency, depending on how fast the means of payment expand. If it should prove to be necessary, its disturbing effects on industry would be much reduced if it went on gradually and steadily, rather than being superimposed upon the customary cyclical expansions and contractions. Under the latter conditions, a long-term downward trend of prices serves to make expansions shorter and contractions longer, and probably more severe. Industry could more easily adjust itself to a slow and fairly regular downward trend.

The increase in product per worker which seems to be potentially available represents lowered unit costs of production, making some reduction of prices quite possible without crippling industry, even if real wages rise, as they naturally would do. The probability is that with the setbacks resulting from depressions largely removed, this process would go on quite as fast as we could find out what to produce in order to make effective use of our increased productive power.

This brings us to the more permanent question of our power to absorb increased productive power in the long run. Here it seems clear that there is no fixed limit to this power, but that, under present conditions, our power to absorb has not kept pace with our power to produce. Power to absorb is in part a matter of purchasing power, but only in part. Real purchasing power is governed not merely by the flow of media of exchange, but also by the prices of goods and services; and its effective character is governed not only by its total amount but by the things for which it is used—its distribution between consumption and savings, between mass-production goods and other goods and services, and between familiar goods and new goods. Equally important is the distribution of potential producing and purchasing power as between more goods and more leisure, and the distribution of the leisure.

But over and above all these questions involved in purchasing power is the problem of producing the right goods in the right proportions, at prices which will cause them to be bought and with adjustments between prices and payments for the factors of production which will enable the producers to go on producing goods in amounts which will utilize all existing factors of production. Production of capital goods has to be adjusted not only to the flow of savings, but to the volume of output for which there is an attainable demand.

It is not merely a question of industry distributing

enough purchasing power to buy its current product at a price consistent with continued production. There must be capacity of increase in the system, and increase at a substantial rate which can be sustained and will not lead to reaction and depression. Out of the current cycle of production and consumption there must flow a volume of purchasing power which will initiate and sustain a larger succeeding cycle, and so on indefinitely. Such an increase can hardly be furnished by endless credit expansion on a fixed currency base, or by any kind of credit expansion flowing mainly to producers. If the expansion of the currency base is not sufficient, lowered prices are required.

It is an unquestionable fact that the present system does not accomplish this task of adjustment successfully; and it is hardly open to question that the mere removal of booms and depressions would not furnish automatic solutions for all the problems of adjustment which would remain. Would the problem be solved if we could by some miracle establish the completely fluid, freely-competitive system of individualistic theory?

To this question no scientifically proven answer can be given. But it seems overwhelmingly probable that under such a system there would still be booms and depressions, though the depressions might be shorter and less serious on the whole than those produced by the present hybrid system. The booms might still never reach our full potential power of production before they exhausted themselves. The net rate of long-run expansion might be faster than the present system permits; but there seems to be no guarantee that it would be as fast as the increase in our power to produce. The processes of adjustment, even under the freest competition imaginable, would still take time and involve uncertainties, errors, and losses.

It should be clearly recognized, also, that "free competition" in this connection means competition which

stands ready to go to unlimited cutthroat lengths whenever necessary to find a market for productive resources
which would otherwise go unused. What this would mean
to modern industry is not entirely easy to visualize; but it
would mean a great many things which the National Recovery Administration and the codes adopted under it are
deliberately trying to do away with, regarding them as
"unfair competition." It would mean revolutionizing the
status of public utility rates and other rigid areas of prices,
remaking financial structures to eliminate fixed charges
(and fixed incomes), and introducing some sort of elasticity into union wage scales, which to organized labor
represent the fruits of many bitter and costly struggles, not
to be given up without still more bitter resistance.

Moves in all these directions are desirable or even necessary to introduce much-needed elasticity into our system;
but that they should go the full lengths required to achieve
the free-competitive ideal is hardly thinkable; especially
in the absence of more definite assurance than can be given
that the net result would be to make us richer in the aggregate instead of poorer.

This brings us face to face with one of the basic faults
in the "price system" as it actually operates: namely, recourse to idleness if production will not cover "costs,"
when these "costs" represent not what the productive resources are worth under existing conditions but what they
would be worth under more favorable conditions than
actually exist. A wage rate of three dollars per day for
making shoes ought to mean that there are other opportunities for using this labor to produce something worth
three dollars per day. If the worker stands idle because he is
not worth three dollars per day at making shoes, that means
that the three-dollar alternative does not exist, or at least
is not available within the limits of existing knowledge.
Under these conditions, to act on the assumption that

shoes are not worth producing unless they will cover the three-dollar wage is false social accounting, flying in the face of the elementary fact that anything produced is that much more than nothing. It stands in the way of our making the best available use of our productive resources, whatever that use may be, by insisting that they shall not be used at all unless their use will cover "costs" which changed conditions may have rendered, for this purpose, arbitrary and misleading. This is a large subject, which the writer has discussed at greater length in his volume entitled *Studies in the Economics of Overhead Costs*.

Under these conditions, it is inevitable that productive resources should go to waste, with the further result that they create no purchasing power to buy the products of other productive resources. And it is quite possible for productive resources to be permanently expelled from the circle of active production and purchase, which becomes adjusted to the shrunken purchasing power resulting from their expulsion and cannot reabsorb them.

Somewhat different is the case of producers who go on producing for next to nothing, and whose purchasing power approaches the zero limit too closely for economic health. Here society at least has the goods they have produced, but it still suffers from a lack of normal balance between its different parts.

At the other extreme from the free-competitive ideal is the completely collectivist system, in which all persons would have a claim to some share of the society's income without reference to whether they were able to contribute to its creation or not. This would dispose of the worst feature of the limited market as a limitation on production, not so much by the money it would give everyone to buy goods with, as by another angle of its effects, which is not so often thought of. It would mean that the extra cost to the employer (the community) of hiring a worker to produce goods as compared to the cost of letting him stand idle would be reduced either to nothing at all or to such a small amount that almost any market demand would suffice to make production worth while. The employer would have little or nothing to gain by limiting output, in the same situation in which the commercial employer is forced to limit it because further production would not cover "out-of-pocket expenses". There would remain, of course, the question of incentives to the workers and to managerial efficiency, the avoidance of bureaucratic stagnation, the method of accumulating adequate capital, and other similar problems familiar enough in the literature of this subject.

Between these two extremes lie those smaller modifications of the existing system which may constitute useful steps of an evolutionary sort, mitigating some of the specific faults in the system. Among these faults are the undue concentration of incomes and probably a resulting tendency to oversaving, though the latter point needs fuller investigation. Any move in the direction of more equal distribution would mean an increased market for the things industry knows how to produce and for which it has spare capacity. If this were achieved mainly at the expense of reducing a volume of savings so swollen that a considerable part of it goes to waste, the change would be very nearly a clear gain.

But methods of working toward this end present dilemmas. A compulsory increase of wages, by increasing costs of production, might lead to restriction of output in the attempt to protect profits—in short, to just the opposite of the desired effect. This is one of the serious dangers to be guarded against in the operation of the National Industrial Recovery Act. It is possible that the wage system in its conventional form cannot solve the dilemma between wage costs low enough to be consistent with full employment, and sufficient progress toward more equal distribution to furnish the type of market which a system of mass production requires, and to avoid the danger of oversaving.

One mitigating factor might be the increase of free social services of various sorts. And one change which could do no harm, and which is necessary if industry is to adjust itself to any real shift which gives wage earners a larger fraction of the social dividend, is a reduction of the spread in costs of production between the most efficient and the least efficient producers.[2] This presents sufficient difficulties, but may not be wholly impossible.

The present writer has a strong prejudice in favor of proceeding by evolutionary methods. If this is to be done, it is not necessary at this time to solve all the problems of long-run adjustment to increased productive power. Measures looking toward stabilization of industrial fluctuations have first claim on our attention. An industrial system which can make substantial progress in this direction will necessarily have developed techniques of coöperative action which may open up possibilities not now in sight for attack on the longer-run problems.

[2]See the concluding paragraphs of the article "Economics and the National Recovery Administration," already referred to.

# III. THE NATURE AND FUNCTIONING OF THE POST-WAR GOLD STANDARD

BY ARTHUR D. GAYER

Despite important differences of detail as between the countries adhering to the gold standard in pre-War days, its underlying principles were everywhere the same. It was characterized by two salient features. The first was the statutory obligation to redeem notes in gold coin. The standard unit of account was defined by statute in terms of a fixed weight of gold of specified fineness. Gold was thus given an invariable price, but its value—its exchange ratio with other goods or purchasing power—was left free to vary with its fluctuating supply and demand. Commercial banks regulated their advances by their cash holdings and these in turn depended upon the gold stocks of central banks. Changes in the price level were, therefore, in the last analysis, the resultant of changes on the one hand in the total volume of the means of payment and the method of their employment, including the velocity of circulation, and changes on the other in the volume of production and trade. The supply of money was thus not deliberately controlled by any central authority to meet the needs of business, but was left to the reputedly automatic regulation of so-called natural forces, most important among them the cost of production of gold. The primary economic function of the gold standard intranationally was thus to place some limit to the supply of money and credit and supposedly to prevent excessive fluctuations in the volume of the total media of payments. Such shortcomings as this arrangement manifested were felt to be a price well worth paying for the freedom it ensured from intervention and possible abuse by political authority.

But the pre-War gold standard also served an international function of regulation. One of its basic foundations was the free movement of gold to and from the industrial arts and the free international movement of gold within the narrow range of the gold points effected through the sensitive mechanism of the foreign exchanges. Indeed, the maintenance of a parity in foreign exchanges within narrow limits was perhaps the chief aim of the international gold standard. The latter demanded from and insured to every country adhering to it not indeed a common price level, but a closely interrelated price and income structure prevailing over the entire gold-standard area; the penalty for divergence of prices in any one country far out of line above the world gold price level being the enforced departure of that country from gold. The currency mechanism itself brought about the restoration of equilibrium, provided certain rules were observed, whenever temporary disequilibrium between any one currency and the rest occurred. For such benefits as each derived from participation in an international system, autonomy of action in domestic monetary policy, except between narrowly restricted limits, was the sacrifice demanded. Thus, though unconsciously, a double preference was implied: first, for such instability of prices as was experienced under the gold standard over the uncertainty and possibly greater instability of a money divorced from a metallic base; and secondly, for stability of international exchanges as compared with possible stability of the internal price level.

An important corollary follows. Any one country could, and still can, under the gold standard, pursue in isolation a deflationary course to its heart's content in opposition to the rest of the world: the only effect will be a piling up of reserves. But the converse is not true. Unless other countries are following the same path, any country which embarks on an inflationary policy or attempts to arrest a process of deflation is subject to the peril of being forced off the gold standard, no matter what its previous accumulation of gold. Recent experience has once again conclusively shown that even abundant gold reserves accumulated in previous periods of prosperity can in these circumstances be rapidly exhausted by an external drain resulting from sudden nervous withdrawals of foreign short-term funds and a flight of capital, as well as by internal hoarding. In other words, central banking authorities must so control the total volume of the media of payments as to prevent or correct an adverse balance of payments and check a resultant gold export. If world gold prices are falling a country has the choice between two and only two courses: to maintain its price level stable above that prevailing abroad at the cost of losing gold and perhaps being forced eventually to abandon the gold base; or to lower its entire internal price and money income structure in line with the fall of world gold prices.

To achieve these ends certain duties have traditionally been regarded as devolving upon central banks. Under an international gold standard the paramount duty of a central bank, to which all other functions are subordinate, is to maintain the currency at par with gold. In order to protect the paper money of the country by redeeming it in gold on demand, central banks must hold the ultimate reserves of the country and make sure that adequate specie or bullion supplies are available. Control over the total volume of the media of payments to effect this end has traditionally been attained by manipulation of the discount rate supplemented and reinforced, if necessary, by the appropriate purchase and sale of securities in so-called open-market operations. When, as is not infrequent, a conflict occurs in the matter of monetary policy between the internal requirements of production and trade and the maintenance of the international exchange value of the currency, the former have to be subordinated to the latter, under the gold standard, for the protection of the gold base. Monetary policy has to be determined not by domestic requirements but by the demand and supply conditions of foreign exchange. Thus the international character of the gold standard, made effective by the free movement of gold, has definite consequences on the maintenance of internal stability. It assures stable parities of exchange by permitting or creating variations in the level of domestic prices. The attempts of various central banks and treasuries since the War to pursue at once, or to reconcile, the two policies of internal stability and stability of the international exchange value of the currency unit have inevitably broken down. For, short of international central-bank coöperation under some modified gold standard which might conceivably combine these two objectives, they are in the last analysis incompatible.[1]

Indeed, it is only in relatively recent times that central banks have learned how to preserve external stability through the mechanism of centralized control of gold movements by using the instruments of discount policy and credit control. The Bank of England, which has systematically practiced such control in one form or another for perhaps a century, has been an exception rather than typical. The deliberate control of gold movements through central bank policy did not emerge in France or Prussia till the eighteen-fifties. In the United States it came into existence only with the establishment of the Federal Reserve System, and in Canada during the War. Even during the present century the tendency of rates to be changed more or less automatically upon variations of gold reserves around a certain conventional amount or percentage ratio to notes

[1] This Special Report embodies certain material from the author's forthcoming study of Monetary Policy and Economic Stabilization, to which the reader is referred for a fuller discussion of the problems treated here.

has held good neither absolutely nor universally. By various means many central banks have attempted to exercise some control over gold movements without alteration of discount rates, while others have held such large reserves that only exceedingly heavy gold losses have necessitated increased rates. Conversely, almost all central banks have tended to some extent to bottle up gold when they received it, without permitting it to exercise its full influence upon the total volume of the means of payment and the general level of prices. In general, however, gold movements prior to the War, by their direct and indirect influences, acted as a corrective of temporary disturbances of international equilibrium. Since the War the principle and practice of control have undergone great extension, but they have been increasing utilized on the contrary to *prevent* gold movements from influencing the internal price structure, with consequences of the utmost importance.

The advantages of the gold standard can be enjoyed only if gold movements are allowed to exercise their full effects on prices and no attempts are made through monetary action to minimize or offset them. One of the cardinal "rules of the gold-standard game" is that the internal price structure should be kept continuously in harmony with and responsive to the external world level. It is the duty of central banks under the gold standard not to protect the domestic credit structure and price level from the repercussions of gold movements, but rather to see that they respond to the latter. Loss of gold demands, not the manufacture of credit to offset it, but credit contraction; conversely, gold imports, unless permitted to have their full influence in raising prices, will sooner or later create maladjustments of a serious nature, if not directly for the country receiving gold, at least for the gold-standard area at large.

In one sense the functioning of the gold standard has

never been wholly automatic, though prior to the War this characterization was better justified than it has been since. For with the growth in all monetary systems of credit superstructures resulting from the development of note issue and deposit banking, constant action on the part of central banks has been needed in controlling the volume of bank credit to correct gold movements in order to preserve the free convertibility of the currency into gold. The very maintenance of convertibility has called for monetary management and in that sense and measure the pre-War gold standard was a managed standard. Management was, and is, demanded under the gold standard merely to keep it such. The differences in management between pre- and post-War years are differences of degree rather than of kind, though in some respects of great magnitude and importance. Yet within these limits of compliance with the "rules of the game" the gold standard may justifiably be designated an automatic standard. The mechanism, however, is often misrepresented by over-simplification. In practice complicated situations often arise not susceptible of easy solution by facile reference to cut and dried rules. Thus, to anticipate problems examined in detail below, if a central bank raises its official rate upon an outflow of gold in order to contract credit, this may in certain circumstances have the effect of attracting both foreign funds and money hoarded domestically in such quantities that the central bank's contraction of credit is compensated by an enlargement of credit granted by commercial banks. Clearly, in these circumstances, which find conspicuous illustration in the United States in the years immediately preceding the Stock Exchange collapse of 1929, the attempt of the central bank to influence the price level through contraction of the total media of payments is frustrated. The converse is true of the situation which may be brought about by gold imports: a lowered discount rate may discourage foreign balances and induce domestic capital to search for more remunerative investment abroad. Such instances, all too often ignored, can easily be multiplied of phenomena which in practice modify the doctrine of free automatism in vital respects.

Thus the characteristic which distinguishes currencies on and off the gold standard, respectively, lies not in monetary management as such but in its object. In the former case there is management, but it has to be directed toward keeping the purchasing power of the currency on an equality with gold. The ultimate responsibility for the domestic price level must always, inevitably, rest with central banks. Under a paper standard, since they enjoy a monopoly in regulating the supply of the means of payment, any purchasing power can be given to the currency; under the gold standard, maintenance of external harmony with the world gold level governs central banks in the exercise of their powers of control. The essential difference between a gold and an inconvertible paper currency is thus that the former has a fixed gold value and a fluctuating purchasing power, while the latter has an indeterminate gold value but may be given any desired purchasing power. The international gold standard affords a mechanism for maintaining stability of exchanges at the price of compelling the internal price and money income structure of each country adhering to it to conform to those of all the others; the reverse being the case with independent currencies cut loose from gold.

Thus a fundamental conflict exists between the principles of the gold standard and a conscious deliberate policy of monetary stabilization. In order that the gold standard should operate efficiently, banking systems should always be "loaned-up"; if central banking authorities are, on the other hand, to enjoy any discretion in monetary policy they must be in possession of surplus reserves. The gold-standard mechanism demands that gold flows should have their full effect alike upon the countries receiving and losing gold; central banks concerned to preserve stability of prices, to mitigate industrial fluctuations, and to avoid creating disturbances in business activity, naturally attempt to counteract these movements by open-market operations. Furthermore, economic developments in the post-War world have made it increasingly clear that the gold standard can no longer be operated upon its original premises. The changes in its structure and functioning which have brought about this condition of affairs must next be examined.

In the nineteenth century general price movements in different countries showed a marked tendency to move harmoniously together over the whole gold-standard area. In the post-War period this process of approximate equalization or at least congruous movement has been prevented from occurring to anything like the same extent by reason of two sets of factors. The first of these "interferences" consists in a considerable departure from the pre-War conception and practice of the gold standard as involving the necessity that gains and losses of gold by central banks should be followed by such monetary policies as will influence the price level and money income structure to the full extent demanded by the increase or diminution of reserves. Pre-War practice rested on the double assumption that countries losing gold would put into effect cheap money policies which would produce a lower level of prices and money incomes, and that countries which were gaining gold would do the reverse. The efforts of central banks in post-War years, however, have been directed in many instances not to seeing that these results were produced, but that they were *prevented* from occurring. Thus the assumptions underlying pre-War practice have frequently not been valid in the post-War world. Instead of gold movements being given their full effect on the price and cost structure, the tendency has often been to *offset* their influence by deliberate measures of *expansion* of bank credit upon the occurrence of a gold outflow and its *contraction* following an inflow. This policy is of course wholly incompatible with the maintenance of the internationally integrated and approximately uniform price and income structure which is the very core of the gold standard. A country which, like the United States, receives gold in consequence of a favorable balance of trade, notwithstanding its heavily creditor position, should in the interests of international equilibrium have a sharply rising level of prices and money incomes. But if it counteracts gold imports by letting its central banking system sell securities and prevent credit expansion, the international readjustment which is required will not take place. Conversely, if gold exports from a country whose internal price-cost structure is too far above the international level, as was the case with Great Britain, are offset by the central bank's creation of credit, again the maladjustments are not corrected. In both cases the policy of internal stabilization may be the more desirable, and indeed in practice the only possible course to pursue, as being a preferable alternative to permitting the price and income structure to rise in the one case, or to fall in the other, to the level demanded for the preservation of international equilibrium. But it is a policy which is utterly at variance with the international integration of domestic price levels which the free flow of gold should bring about.

The second of the two factors in the post-War world which have prevented gold movements from producing an approximate equalization of prices is the increasing extent to which economic structures have offered resistance to monetary policies and prevented them from achieving their objective, when necessary in raising, but more particularly in lowering the money income level. A flexible price level moved up and down by monetary policy in response to fluid gold movements demands a flexible cost structure. If the pressure or relaxation exerted by credit restriction or expansion is not passed down all along the line to the different factors of production in due proportions, its effects are obstructed and maladjustments of one kind or another are bound to develop. The extent to which increasing rigidities of the economic structure have developed in the post-War decade has fundamentally altered the whole problem and necessitates reëxamination of the basic premises on which the pre-War gold standard rested.

Yet it was not so easy to put pre-War principles into practice in the post-War world. Consider the case of Great Britain. During the period after 1925 the British price structure was clearly out of equilibrium with the world level, as a result in large measure of the initial overvaluation of sterling at the time the gold standard was restored. London was in consequence exposed to the persistent threat of a net export of gold. Yet no appropriate contraction of credit was effected. The Deputy Governor of the Bank of England later stated:

You will find, if you look at a succession of Bank returns, that the amount of gold we have lost has been almost entirely replaced by an increase in the Bank's securities.[2]

Yet can anyone doubt, in view of the magnitude of the difficulties involved in the reduction to a lower level of the internal cost structure, and especially of wage rates, that the alternative "orthodox" policy could not have been carried out without provoking disastrous social consequences? Here domestic non-monetary factors offered the most stubborn sort of resistance to the effects which should have followed the application of traditional monetary measures for the correction of internal disequilibrium with the international situation.

[2] *Minutes of Evidence before British Committee on Finance and Industry* (The "Macmillan" Committee), Vol. I, Question 353.

But it is to the United States that we must turn if we would see most clearly illustrated the absurd conclusions to which we are led by the demand for pre-War orthodoxy in the operation of the gold standard in the changed conditions of the post-War world. Those who condemn the pre-depression policy of the Federal Reserve authorities in their departure from gold-standard orthodoxy should in consistency realize that these principles would have required that an inflationary boom of probably much larger proportions should have been allowed to develop at certainly a much earlier date. For America had a greatly excessive gold stock and on pre-War principles should have permitted it to have its full influence in raising prices. In no other way could she, with her high tariff wall, or possibly even without it, have developed a sufficiently large adverse balance of trade to relieve her of her surplus gold. The critics of the post-War, pre-depression "stabilization" policy of the Federal Reserve Board, which was certainly not free from serious errors, cannot have it both ways. If monetary "management" is wrong in principle, the Federal Reserve Board should have refrained from all active "interference," and desisting from "artificial" attempts to control the price level, should have allowed it to soar upwards to the full extent justified by the gold reserves, to a point where the process was arrested by the growth in volume of foreign imports. It is unreasonable to demand on the one hand that the Federal Reserve System should, on pre-War central banking principles, have refrained from practicing deliberate control of the price level, and on the other that it should on post-War principles have ignored, as indeed it largely did, the historic index of the reserves and exercised *more* credit control to prevent the development of a boom. In fine, on pre-War theory of the full utilization of gold reserves we should have had not less, but more inflation between 1921 and 1929. This is quite apart from the effects, mentioned above, which attempts to control the volume of credit in response to gold movements by means of discount rate manipulation are quite likely to have: a rise in bank rates attracting, a fall driving away, short-term liquid funds in excessive volume, thus frustrating all influence exerted on the price level.

The reciprocal influences of gold movements and changing price levels on each other constitute the basic article in the dogma of the automatic functioning of the gold standard. In post-War years, however, the great growth in the accumulation and international flow of short-term capital, and the circumstance that the world is financially more closely knit than in pre-War days, have had the effect of much weakening this connection.

Today the inflow or outflow of gold, by causing a raising or lowering of the price of discount credit, causes such a rapid and considerable shifting of the liquid funds on the world money market that the direction of the movement of gold is bound to change *before any alteration in the price level can take place*. . . . The classic contention that "the export of gold means a fall in prices" has become an anachronism. Today a change in the price of credit alone suffices, not merely to check the inflow or outflow of gold, but to change an outflow into an inflow or *vice versa*. The dearness of credit attracts foreign capital like a magnet . . . Under present conditions, a Central Bank must operate by means of a strong credit policy maintained over a fairly long period, if it wishes to influence the level of prices. . . . The gold standard now is, and must be in an increasing degree, a manipulated standard . . . The movement of gold, the volume and price of credit and the changes in price levels have lost their mutual correlation. Harmony has given place to discord.[3]

Under the post-War operation of the gold standard the

[3]Dr. Feliks Mlynarski, *The Functioning of the Gold Standard* (memorandum submitted to the Gold Delegation of the Financial Committee of the League of Nations), pp. 15-17. When the discount rate was raised in the United States in 1928, the amount of bank acceptances purchased by foreign central banks increased by over two hundred million dollars in six months. Conversely the Bank of England experienced a large and rapid withdrawal of deposits whenever it lowered its rates below that of the Federal Reserve banks. (*Ibid*, p. 19.)

international leveling of prices demanded by the gold standard no longer takes place automatically through the influence of gold movements, if it is effected at all, and domestic price levels have in consequence become increasingly independent of one another. The internationally interrelated price and money income structure ruling throughout the entire area of the gold standard has been becoming a myth in the post-War world. Before the crisis, local price levels, instead of moving up and down together, moved at certain periods upwards in some countries, down in others, and in others again remained stable.

The pre-War connection between international gold flows and local price levels has been weakened in another important respect by the great extension of the gold-exchange standard system. This device possesses the very great merit of reducing the world's monetary demand for gold by the inclusion in central bank reserves of foreign exchange convertible into gold at will. In practice, except in times of panic, the foreign exchange is not so converted. But it may be, and often is, easily transferred from one center to another, especially if, as we have seen, higher money rates attract it elsewhere. But in their effects on price levels such international movements of short-term liquid funds differ radically from international gold movements. International gold movements, if not counteracted by central banking policy, have an influence on the price levels of both the country losing and the country receiving the gold. Shifting liquid balances, in contrast, have a one-sided effect. The reciprocal effect of the transference of central banking reserves has been distorted. Credit in the country of a central bank acquiring or losing foreign exchange may be respectively relaxed or restricted, but no corresponding effect need be felt upon the credit structure of the country from which the balances are being withdrawn or in which they are deposited. If these foreign exchange reserves were concentrated in foreign central banks this might not happen: the supreme banking authorities would be in a position to take such action as was deemed appropriate upon their increase or diminution. But in actual practice it is with the commercial banks that these funds are mainly deposited. This latter fact aggravates the disturbance they are likely to create and constitutes another disadvantage of the gold-exchange standard. Large accumulations of foreign short-term balances by foreign countries applying the gold-exchange standard are a strain upon and a threat to the great monetary centers where they are deposited, inasmuch as they can be turned into gold or transferred elsewhere without warning. In order to protect themselves against this danger and to be prepared for emergencies, the central banks of these world money markets have been compelled to keep larger gold reserves than they would otherwise have needed, thus to some extent offsetting the economies in the use of gold effected by the gold-exchange standard mechanism itself.

These abnormally large amounts of internationally held liquid capital have not merely generated international uncertainty and instability instead of performing their traditional functions of correcting, through gold movements, international disparities in price levels. They have also led to internal instability and confusion, as a result of the effects upon the reserve base produced by gold imports, but more especially by gold exports. When large and rapid foreign gold drains occur in nervous situations, they can provoke domestic alarm and apprehension which find expression in internal hoarding of gold and currency. The acute sensitivity of short-term capital in post-War years and its abnormal volume have tended to aggravate gold flows and have often set in motion a train of consequences cumulative in their effect. This has been as true of periods of rising prices and expansion as of periods of deflation.

For, as shown above, a rise of prices in any one country, whether of commodities or securities, may not have the effect of inducing the gold export which, according to classic monetary theory, should result and thus restore equilibrium by bringing prices down again. Its effect may instead be to attract capital and produce a gold inflow which encourages prices to rise still higher, as happened in the New York stock market boom of 1928-29. The reverse sequence holds good of periods of falling prices. In such conditions monetary policy can hardly consist in mechanical reflex action regulated by gold movements along traditional lines: deliberate management becomes inevitable. The problem is not as simple as orthodox theory has represented it, and the responsibility for conscious control of credit, price levels, and gold flows cannot be evaded.

Such success as the international gold standard enjoyed in pre-War days was in large measure attributable to the international commercial and financial dominance of one country, Great Britain. By reason of the immense volume of her foreign investments and the conservatism, allied to an absence of political pressure, with which they were made; the complete freedom of her gold and foreign exchange markets; her whole-hearted adherence to the principle and practice of free trade in goods; and lastly the freedom of the Bank of England from interference from the Treasury, Great Britain enjoyed a position of undisputed leadership and power in the operation of the gold standard. For the half century before the War London's predominance in the world's financial markets rendered the value of gold and the value of sterling virtually synonymous: sterling was indeed the international standard.

England's relative decline in international trade and finance has introduced an element of uncertainty and confusion into the situation. As no other center has been qualified to assume London's rôle of unchallenged supremacy, there have been in recent years, in place of one, three great world financial centers which in their administration of the gold standard have often pulled in opposite directions and worked at cross purposes, and which have offered the choice between three depositaries for mobile short-term balances.

Great Britain employed her international lending power as the world's leading creditor country in a manner consistent with the requirements of this position. The two countries which, largely by the fortunes of war, fell heir to the ground she lost, namely the United States and France, have signally failed, partly by reason of inexperience, partly by force of circumstances, to utilize their creditor power similarly in the purchase of additional foreign products in appropriate volume or in making additional foreign loans on long-term in a continuous stream, with caution and on the basis of economic expectations alone. On the contrary, whereas England operated on an extraordinarily small gold reserve, they have taken a large part of their annual surplus in gold or in short-term liquid claims. As regards foreign investment, one of the two, France, has shown, for a variety of not incomprehensible reasons, great reluctance to lend abroad on long-term, lending instead on short-term to a disproportionate extent. She has in addition been influenced in her foreign lending by non-financial considerations of a diplomatic sort which have rendered her an uncertain creditor and made the movement of French balances quite incalculable. The United States, on the other hand, has exercised her power to lend abroad spasmodically, by violent fits and starts, and with great imprudence. Both countries have been influenced, moreover, by isolationist sentiments which have militated against the smooth working of an international standard.

It is hardly necessary to stress yet once again the self-contradictory policy pursued by the United States in insisting on the payment of war debts—which must have created confusion in the best of circumstances, since these large payments did not represent earnings of productive investments—while she prevented by her tariff barriers their payment in the only possible way in which it could have been made; the injury which this course of action inflicted on the world at large ultimately engulfing her too. The method whereby the United States was enabled to continue so long her anomalous rôle of a creditor on large scale which yet enjoyed a favorable balance of trade was through a tremendous process of foreign lending, much of which was grossly improvident and the proceeds of which were used in some measure by the borrowers for non-productive purposes. From the point of view both of her own interests and of those of the world at large, the United States has shown herself a most unsatisfactory creditor country. She has functioned vigorously in this respect only intermittently, unlike London in pre-War days, which could be relied upon to distribute capital throughout the world in a fairly steady flow. In the supply of and demand for short-term accommodation her influence has also been disturbingly sporadic as a result of stock market booms and the attraction they have exercised on foreign liquid capital. Till 1928 the volume of foreign loans floated in New York kept increasing: then that source of foreign borrowing, which had come to be regarded as permanently available, suddenly began to dry up. American capital issues for foreign account dropped from 841 million dollars in the first half of 1928 to 409 million dollars in the second half of that year and to 218 million dollars in the second half of 1929.[4] American and French influences together have rendered the flow of world capital for foreign investment

[4]*Report of the Gold Delegation*, p. 19, para. 50. (Corrected figures.)

much more irregular than before the War, when Britain played so large a part in its total international movement, with effects upon both borrowers and lenders proportionately disturbing.

To sum up: since the War it has become an anachronism to speak of the automatic functioning of the gold standard; the gold standard has become a managed currency. The question is no longer whether we shall have monetary management, but what sort of monetary management we shall have. Since there must be monetary control the only choice is between good and bad, deliberate and unintentional control. It has ceased to be possible to have "automatic" control. The supporting foundations of a free uncontrolled gold standard have long ago been sapped beyond repair. Gold movements have been determined more often than not by changes in interest rates rather than by relative changes in price levels. Central banks have regulated domestic price structures largely independently of gold flows. In the United States particularly the connection between the gold reserve and the credit superstructure has been increasingly ignored. In the pre-War sense we have not been on the gold standard since the War, though we have had a currency amply covered by gold. The Federal Reserve's management of currency and credit has determined rather than been determined by the changing value of gold. By the consistent utilization of the devices of "off-setting" and "sterilizing," which the United States was in a position to practice by virtue of her huge gold stocks, the total media of payments have been regulated independently of her reserves and to suit supposed domestic business needs. The value of gold has been the value arbitrarily given the dollar by the American monetary authorities. The international gold standard in the post-War decade up to 1929 was in reality an international standard based upon the dollar. Similarly, in the case of Great Britain, gold flows have been prevented from exercising their full effect on the domestic price and money income structure. The speedy communication of impulses from without to national economic structures has been increasingly impeded by deliberate action dictated by the force of circumstances, with the result that gold has not been permitted to perform its essential function of enforcing international equilibrium and establishing a single internationally integrated price and income structure over the whole gold-standard area. The non-monetary factors which have been largely responsible for this development are examined in Special Report IV.

# IV. NON-MONETARY FACTORS AFFECTING THE FUNCTIONING OF THE POST-WAR GOLD STANDARD

## BY ARTHUR D. GAYER

The difficulties under which the gold standard has functioned in post-War years have been only partly due to the changes in internal structure, discussed in Special Report III, which it has undergone. Equally or more important have been the non-monetary changes in the conditioning economic environment in and through which any monetary standard has to function. The gold standard is at bottom a monetary instrument demanding flexibility of economic structures, but since the War it has been operating in a world of growing economic rigidities.[1] Whether the fault lies with the gold standard itself or with attempts at artificial control of economic factors, there can be no difference of opinion that either the monetary mechanism must conform to the nature of its economic environment, or the environment be adapted to the needs of the monetary standard. The question, however, is not so much whether in theory it is ideally preferable to force economic activity to proceed flexibly in the Procrustean bed of an automatic international monetary system such as the gold standard, or whether to fashion the monetary system to fit the unyielding framework of a relatively rigid economic structure. In theory, under ideal conditions, either alternative would do equally well. The question, rather, is this: which end is more easily attainable without producing undesirable social and economic consequences—whether to attempt

[1] The problems discussed in this Special Report are treated at greater length in the author's forthcoming study of Monetary Policy and Economic Stabilization, certain material from which is embodied here.

to reverse the apparent tendency of economic development in recent decades, or to modify or change our monetary system?

A régime of relatively free competition, domestically and internationally, with mobility not only of goods but also, in reasonable measure, of labor, is indispensable for the smooth and semi-automatic functioning of the gold standard. A completely competitive régime has of course never existed. It is a methodologically useful fiction when recognized as such and created for speculative purposes; one which can be employed without danger provided that we remember that deductions based on this simplified caricature are not applicable to real life without further ado. Yet in the nineteenth century free competition did play so much greater a part in regulating economic life than it does today that we are justified in loosely characterizing the system as it then existed as one of free competitive enterprise, and of treating obstructions to the natural play of economic forces as so many exceptions to the rule rather than as the rule itself. It is questionable if this assumption is any longer justifiable in the post-War world of the twentieth century.

Since the War, and indeed ever since the pure philosophy of economic individualism began to wane during the latter decades of the nineteenth century, the tendency has been for the economic system to be subjected to an increasing degree of conscious direction and control, both as a whole and in its component parts. The instances which immediately spring to mind are numerous, obvious, and familiar. They fall roughly into two classes: those resulting from the assumption by the State of an ever-widening range of economic functions, governments having to an increasingly large extent themselves undertaken or attempted to regulate or guide certain types of economic activity; and, on the other hand, the efforts which private business itself has exerted to exercise artificial control over prices, output, conditions of production, etc., in the interest of larger returns than those yielded by free competition. Thus, apart from the effect of the variety of unavoidable frictions inherent in the functioning of all human institutions, the processes of pure or perfect competition have encountered an increasingly large degree of interference imposed both from without by public authority and from within by industry itself. Some types of control fall into both categories, or cut across this division. The result has been that the monetary mechanism, in effecting readjustments and correcting disequilibria, has met resistances, both national and international, in considerable areas of the price structure which have been rendered inflexible by governmental regulation and large-scale organization both of capital and labor: rigidities in wage rates and in certain commodity prices, railroad and public utility rates, social service costs, the salaries of public officials, and a widening range of contractual obligations. These factors will be briefly considered in succession.

The direct and indirect charges on industry which are fixed by contract have grown much heavier in recent decades as a result of the increasing variety of economic services which the state has been performing. The inflexibility of these charges is not equally great in all cases. Most rigid of all are payments unalterably fixed in terms of money over a long period of years, such as interest on long-term government securities, except where this can be reduced by debt conversion operations. The importance of this factor has grown since the War in proportion to the vast increase in the indebtedness of governments, both central and local, throughout the world. There is no way of permanently reducing this element of rigidity short of reducing the magnitude of public debt from its present high level. The possibility of so doing depends in turn upon the extent to which governments can, and should, permanently cut down their expenditures by divesting themselves of many of the additional functions which they have been discharging in recent years, or alternatively can have recourse in larger measure to a pay-as-you-go policy of financing out of tax receipts. These observations apply equally, *mutatis mutandis*, to the fixed interest-bearing securities of private enterprise.

Only less rigid are many types of payment which are not contractual in the same sense as interest on bonded debt, but which are fixed by statute or custom. Into this category fall disbursements under unemployment insurance systems, public health services, pension schemes, and the like. Though the scale of these social service charges has hitherto been relatively greater in many European countries than in the United States, their rapid extension here also must be expected, a prospect which will be welcomed by most for social and humanitarian reasons even when not on strictly economic grounds. The stubborn resistance likely to be offered to any downward revision in these charges is sufficiently clearly illustrated by recent European, and particularly British, experience. Once introduced, here is an element of inflexibility which can be reduced only with the greatest difficulty and at the risk of provoking widespread popular discontent and disturbance.

Another inelastic factor is found in the salaries of public officials. Inasmuch as these are based on long-term calculations of governments and long-range expectations on the part of those entering the civil services, they cannot be easily given greater flexibility. Reductions can, it is true, be effected in periods of depression without much difficulty, because the recipients are relatively powerless to resist them; but this practice cannot often be repeated without detriment to the public interest, because the caliber of the personnel attracted and hence the quality of public administration is likely in the long run to suffer deterioration. Greater flexibility in this respect is not desirable unless it means more flexible upward, as well as downward, movement in response to cyclical changes in business activity.

These are only a few examples of rigidities which it would be very difficult to reduce. The greatest opportunities for introducing more elasticity into public expenditures, provided comprehensive long-range plans to that end are carefully formulated well in advance, lie in capital outlays on permanent public improvements being undertaken on a flexible schedule. But here it is emphatically not in the interests of economic balance that public works expenditures should be reduced in periods of depression and expanded in boom times. For such a policy would have the effect during booms of intensifying inflationary tendencies by increasing the pressure on the supply of labor and materials, and conversely of deepening the severity of depressions by reinforcing the decline in private spending by a curtailment of public expenditure. Rather should the volume of public works be so controlled as to vary in the *opposite* direction to the fluctuations in private business in order to offset them and thus serve as a compensating force.

Since the great bulk of wage payments is disbursed by private enterprise on short-period terms, the same problem does not arise in connection with them as in the case of contractual obligations or those fixed by law and custom for relatively long periods. Yet the popular resistance to downward revision of wage scales in periods of falling prices is notorious, and even where it can be successfully accomplished the social friction engendered is likely to be considerable. The difficulty is especially great where strong labor unions exist to offer organized opposition. In their absence, on the other hand, the difficulty lies in pushing up wage levels rapidly enough in periods of rising prices, because of the opposition of employers. This is an equally great evil from the point of view of flexibility of the price structure, inasmuch as the excessive profits which result encourage inflationary over-expansion with subsequent reaction into depression. Those who demand greater flexibility of wage rates in periods of declining economic activity—meaning thereby less resistance to reductions—should in logical consistency remember that, if flexibility is a virtue, less time-lag in the rise of wages on the upswing of the cycle, so that maladjustments may be prevented from developing, is every bit as desirable; and they should be prepared to show how this greater flexibility of movement in *both* directions is to be secured. The ill effects likely to result from relatively inflexible wage rates combined with fluid profit margins find equally good illustration in the opposite experiences of Great Britain and the United States during the years 1925-1929. The relative stagnation and abnormal unemployment suffered by the former after her return to gold at the pre-War parity of exchange were due in at least large part to the difficulty encountered in reducing wages in proportion to the increased value of sterling and to the extent necessary for Britain to recapture her quota of world foreign trade. On the other hand the development of the boom in the United States during this period must be partly attributed to the failure of wages to rise sufficiently to compensate, under a relatively stable wholesale price level, for rapid reductions in unit costs of production, and thus to keep profits in check.

Space does not permit a discussion of the problem of the extent of monopoly and quasi-monopoly control over the prices of raw and manufactured products and of certain services, conspicuously those of railroads and public utilities: it need only be remarked that despite a succession of "anti-trust" measures in the United States the range of products and services falling into this class has grown steadily wider. Right through the first three years of the depression the price of certain steel products, for instance, fell hardly at all. The same is true of most public utility rates, while railroad rates were actually raised in some instances. Numerous similar examples could be cited from other countries, Germany in particular, of the prices of cartelized products being increased when the general level of prices was falling.

The subject is too familiar to need elaboration. The point of importance is that this sort of partial price stabilization is worse than no price stability at all, because it throws the entire burden of the readjustment made necessary by any shift in the general price level upon the remaining area of uncontrolled flexible prices, thereby greatly intensifying their fluctuation and creating violent disequilibrium throughout the whole price structure. Such stability of individual prices in certain limited areas during the transition from one general level of prices to another is purchased, however, at the cost not only of greater price instability elsewhere, but also of instability of output and employment in the industries which produce the controlled articles. Conditions in steel may again be instanced as a case in point.

The same is true of products controlled under international cartels, pools, valorization schemes, and the like. Attempts at the artificial control of the supply of many raw materials—wheat, sugar, coffee, rubber, silk, silver, copper—have prevented the natural adjustment of prices to underlying changes in conditions of demand and supply, and rendered them unresponsive to movements in the general price level. The fact that these interferences have in the past failed to maintain themselves permanently has served only to make the ensuing collapse all the worse. Though such price-supporting measures tend to break down in periods of sufficiently severe business decline, the problem is how to prevent their formation at other times so that the continuance and extension of over-production leading to subsequent violent collapse may not be encouraged. The effect of all these operations, which have taken a great variety of form, is to impair the safety and usefulness of the organized machinery of the commodity markets, whether undertaken by governments or by private interests. They make doubly difficult the rational prediction, upon the basis of statistical information, of the probable future behavior of prices, and so weaken one of the basic supports of a freely competitive system.

The gold standard cannot function properly unless the international movement of goods, as well as their internal exchange, enjoys a reasonable degree of freedom from restraints. Tariff barriers destroy the relatively uniform world price level the establishment of which is at once the virtue of and a necessity for the gold standard. But during post-War years the price levels of different countries have been growing more local. The varied restrictions placed upon the free international flow of goods have become not less but more unsurmountable. From the point of view of pure economic theory, which irrefutably demonstrates the advantages of free trade under the flexible competitive conditions it assumes, this tendency, fundamentally inconsistent as it is with the needs of an international monetary system, must be regarded as retrogressive and vicious. Since, however, it exists and shows no signs of waning, it must be recognized and reckoned with. But to attribute the victorious growth of tariffs and trade barriers, on the basis of free trade sympathies rooted in the nineteenth-century classicist economics, solely to the selfish pressure of the sectional interests likely to be benefited by them is too superficial an analysis and misses an important point. Unquestioned and deplorable as is the existence of these factors, there is a deeper explanation for their surprising success in the post-War world.

This has been the desire of individual countries to get their foreign balances into proper equilibrium with their general economic conditions, these somewhat crude artificial means being employed both because the international mechanism through which equilibrium was established in pre-War days has no longer functioned satisfactorily, and because of the increasing difficulty which has been encountered in making the necessary internal adjustments required by changing external circumstances. Tariffs and trade barriers have, in other words, been utilized to some extent because other adequate methods of control for the correction of maladjustments have not been available, and because equilibrium was no longer being established by the free play of unimpeded economic forces. If this analysis does not apply to the post-War tariff history of the United States, it does fit the case of Great Britain, who forsook her traditional free-trade policy reluctantly and adopted restrictive measures as a means of self-protection. The growth of so many rigidities and interferences imposed both from within the national economy and from without by other nations made recourse inevitable to such counter controls as were available. No country can tolerate being at the mercy of world forces working out, automatically or under the influence of other countries, an equilibrium which is not in harmony with its own peculiar conditions and to which it has not the elasticity to adapt itself. A large measure of freedom from outside interferences which make themselves felt through an international monetary system may be necessary for the pursuit of social and economic ends which are deemed desirable nationally but conflict with world trends. Some sacrifice of the benefits of full participation in a completely international system might in these circumstances reasonably be regarded as a price worth paying. It is here, and not in crude protectionist fallacies of the popular sort, that are to be partly found the deeper roots of what must otherwise appear the inexplicable movement toward national self-sufficiency and economic isolation so rampant since the War. Such considerations have nothing in common with discredited protectionist doctrines, but transcend that historic controversy. The partial justification of restrictions on international trade in the modern world is the free hand which a nation is likely to find indispensable when carrying out great social and economic experiments such as the one which is proceeding under our eyes in the United States today. One need not ask how compatible a substantial general lowering of American tariff barriers would be with the necessities of the economic transformation which is being attempted under the Industrial Recovery and the Agricultural Adjustment Acts while these experiments are still in process of being implemented.

The course of events during the depression has shown in their clearest light the real motives and purposes which have inspired the imposition of tariffs, import quotas, exchange restrictions, and the rest. It was concern to restrain trade sufficiently to reduce excessive foreign payments in gold. The imposition of the restrictions was for the defense of the country's currency. While they are certainly causes of the destruction of international trade and of deepening depression, they are yet at the same time symptoms and results of international tension. It is characteristic of an automatic competitive system that each separate nation—just like each business concern within each nation—is individually powerless to refrain from such mutually injurious policies, but is compelled rather to resort to them in self-defense. *In the long run*, it is true, such measures are unnecessary, but only *providing that the necessary internal adjustments can be made without intolerable strain* and without provoking undesirable social and economic friction. Tariffs interfere with the working of international trade, but they may facilitate as well as retard the establishment of international equilibrium, and even be essential to the maintenance of the gold standard.

The ultimate ideal of those who emphasize the need of flexibility in the economic system is a world in which individual prices are so fluid that they would all move up and down promptly and in unison in response to any changes in general economic conditions. In such a world, movements in the general level of prices would be of no consequence, since they would cause no disturbance in the internal relations between particular prices within the total cost-price structure which, by exaggerating or impairing actual or prospective profits, are the root cause of all the trouble.

A moment may be well spent in examining the logical implications of this conception of a completely elastic system. In the first place, as shown above, it would stress the need for greater flexibility of movement in certain individual elements equally in both the upward and downward direction. If the "stickiness" of these factors is harmful during the declining phase of the cycle in preventing necessary readjustments, their tendency to lag is just as injurious on the upswing, though the evil effects are not seen at the time, since maladjustments are permitted to develop. Demonstration of the need for reductions all along the line during depressions is not sufficient: it is necessary to show also how corresponding increases are to be effected during periods of expansion.

In the second place, greater flexibility should mean greater flexibility throughout the entire price structure: it should apply to all elements, not merely to a few selected ones. Obvious though this observation sounds, the advocacy of greater flexibility has in the past too often boiled down in practice to a one-sided demand for wage cuts during depressions and thus has amounted to a defense of other inflexible elements at the expense of labor. But if increased flexibility is to be understood as meaning increased *general* flexibility it should imply during periods of severe price decline a drastic writing-down of capital liabilities, unimpeded by any government interference designed to mitigate this ruthless but rapid process of liquidation through wholesale bankruptcy and foreclosure, alike in the manufacturing, agricultural, and financial spheres, regardless of social consequences. Rather, on these principles, should the government, if it intervenes at all, do so for the purpose of encouraging and expediting this process. Those who argued for thoroughgoing deflation throughout the entire price-cost-debt structure during the depression before our abandonment of gold were at least logically consistent, however limited was their perception of social realities. For a policy of genuine balanced deflation, which aims at bringing costs below prices, and one of inflation, aimed at raising prices above costs, have more in common with each other (since both seek to establish proper internal relations in the cost and price structure), than either has with the attempt to ride two horses at once or alternately. Nothing could be more inconsistent and doomed to failure than a policy of deflating with one hand by reducing wages, refusing assistance for unemployment relief out of public treasuries, and curtailing public works expenditures, while simultaneously preventing deflation by supporting with public funds the weaker banks, railroads, and insurance companies. Elasticity in the economic system should imply at such times a deflation not only of wages but also of capital structures, even if this involves the widespread collapse of big businesses, railroads, insurance companies, and savings banks. It should also mean leaving the farmers to their fate, and allowing nature and the law to take their course—provided the farmers do not resist nature by taking the law into their own hand!

Finally we must consider not only what sort of economic

flexibility is desirable, but how far we may reasonably hope to bring it about in actual practice under conditions as they are. We must take the world largely as we find it, and make the best of it we can, however much more desirable some other kind of world may appear to be, if it is unattainable. When the various elements of rigidity existing in our economic system today are passed one by one in review, even as rapidly as was done above, the possibility of their being mitigated without doing more harm than good is seen to be rather slender, and this quite apart from those rigidities which by their very nature are ineliminable because inherent in our type of economic order.

The other reason for the growing rigidity of economic processes in the modern world is found in their increasing complexity—the "lengthening" of the processes of production and the increasing interval between the first step and the last. This development is a characteristic and concomitant of economic advance. The successive stages of transformation through which goods have to pass before they reach the final consumer have become more numerous, more complicated, and in the aggregate more time-consuming. This is merely another way of saying that the accumulated stock of capital equipment with which production is carried on grows *pari passu* with and is a measure of economic progress: the productive process has become what has been described as more "roundabout." But a flexible economic system demands not only flexibility of prices, but flexibility of the "real" factors whose demand and supply are pivoted upon and guided by price movements. It requires, in other words, that productive factors should be easily transferable from one use to another, that productive resources, both capital and labor, should be easily diverted from one channel into another, the losses incurred by the capitalists being taken promptly, and labor moving fluidly to other occupations. With the growth of fixed capital and the increasing specialization of labor this transference is becoming not less, but more, difficult and painful to effect.

Finally, the vision of an elastic system responding freely in all its component parts to movements in the general price level, and promptly making the necessary readjustments, wholly ignores inelasticities of demand and supply which are not due to "institutional frictions" and the resistance offered by human contrivances, but are rooted in the productive technique and organization of the processes involved. The production of raw materials and foodstuffs is a conspicuous case in point of output which cannot by its nature respond promptly to changes in prices. It requires years for the adjustment to be made. A falling demand for manufactured products is met by a reduction of output which goes some way toward mitigating the severity of the drop in price. But agricultural production cannot in such circumstances be quickly curtailed; and the drop in price is made all the more precipitous by reason of the fact that all demand schedules expressed in terms of money move to the left in periods of a generally declining price level. Space does not permit a discussion here of the technical aspects of this problem; but the familiar phenomenon of a glut of agricultural products in depressions is sufficient evidence of the failure of output to make the prompt response to price movements required by the doctrine of flexible adjustments. In the short run, production is quite likely to be actually increased rather than curtailed, especially by predominantly agricultural and debtor countries in their desperate efforts to keep up the value of their exports sufficiently to cover their imports and payment of debt charges, thus depressing world prices still further and setting up a vicious circle from which the only way of escape is through financial collapse or at least the abandonment of the gold standard. This is just one example of a whole range of ineradicable inflexibilities which the advocates of an elastic system tend to pass over too lightly.

# V. MONETARY POLICY AND PUBLIC WORKS

BY ARTHUR D. GAYER

In recent years proposals for utilizing public works as an agency of economic stabilization in an unstable economic system have been receiving much attention. In essence, the suggestion is that public works should be planned and budgeted sufficiently far in advance to allow them to be conducted on a flexible schedule, operations being timed to fluctuate inversely with general cyclical movements of business, that is, retarded in periods of prosperity and speeded in times of industrial stagnation. In the past public works have usually tended to be undertaken in large volume in good times, both because of increased popular demand and because governments have the necessary revenue or are more willing to borrow. Conversely, depressions have usually found public authorities with a heavy load of debt and impaired borrowing powers. Thus the expansion of public construction in prosperity has increased the pressure on the market for materials and the labor supply, and consequently has encouraged inflationary tendencies; while its contraction in periods of depression has reinforced the reduction of private spending by a curtailment of public expenditures. It is argued that an elastic system of controlled public works would correct both these evils by giving when needed a general stimulus or check to economic activity as a whole.

The success of a policy of controlled public works depends largely upon the relative volume which can be conducted on a flexible schedule. Not all public works can be readily advanced or postponed. The degree in which this is feasible depends in turn upon the thoroughness with which advance plans have been prepared, and upon almost infinitely varied local conditions, but perhaps fifty per cent could be so reallocated. The long-range planning and budgeting of public works is, however, an essential prerequisite if a great variety of unavoidable administrative, technical, and financial difficulties of a very time-consuming character are to be successfully surmounted.

The criticism is sometimes raised that the greatest possible increase in public works would not be sufficiently large to offset variations in private building, much less of industry in general, as between years of prosperity and depression. The following figures throw some light on the problem.

Aggregate annual expenditures for all public construction purposes, Federal, state, and local, throughout the United States, increased steadily from two and a quarter billion dollars in 1923 to over three and a half billions in each of the years 1927 to 1930. Thereafter they fell sharply to two billions in 1932.[1] On the other hand, total Federal expenditures (included in the above figures) for new construction, repairs, and alterations, but excluding floating equipment and aircraft, rose sharply, as a result of the Federal government's success both in speeding its own projects and increasing its road-building grants to the states, from 325 million dollars in 1930 to over 560 millions in 1932 (fiscal years), in contrast to an average annual increase of about 18 million dollars between 1923 and 1930.

Total construction expenditures, public and private, declined from over ten billion dollars in 1928 to about four billion dollars in 1932. Allowing for the decrease in construction costs in the interval, this is equivalent to a fall in their physical volume from 100 to about 55. Had local authorities, state, county, and city, expanded their con-

[1]For detailed figures, and their sources, see the author's article on "Public Works" in the *Encyclopædia of the Social Sciences*, certain material from which is embodied in this report.

struction expenditures as greatly as did the Federal government during the depression, the dollar value of construction would have remained almost constant while the physical volume would have increased. But granting that this would be expecting too much, the effectiveness of the device depends less upon the amount of the increase or decrease than upon its correct timing. An expansion or contraction of public works at the appropriate moment, whenever that might happen to occur (a question considered below), could have an influence upon business in general out of all proportion to its magnitude. Many incidental benefits would also accrue. Government agencies would gain greatly by planning and undertaking their public improvements in orderly sequences instead of haphazardly. Building costs are usually lower in periods of depression: between 1928 and 1932 they fell in the ratio of 100 to 70 or 75. Finally, borrowing at reasonable rates is also usually easier, provided that—an important proviso—the credit of the government unit in question has not been weakened by excessive borrowing in times of prosperity. Even if under the most favorable conditions a flexible public works policy could not eliminate all cyclical fluctuations, were this desirable, it still might succeed in mitigating their violence.

Figures of construction employment in the United States are notoriously inadequate, and no accurate measure is possible of the numbers engaged directly or indirectly on public construction. Estimates differ markedly, but various counts and series of incomplete coverage would seem to indicate that perhaps 800,000 were employed directly on all public construction during the years 1927 to 1930. In addition it has been computed that for each worker employed directly on public construction perhaps two are given employment indirectly in the manufacture and transportation of building materials and equipment. Moreover, there is the still further employment created as a result of the demand exercised by these workers for consumers' goods. This "secondary" employment thus created by public works during depressions has been calculated to be perhaps roughly as large again, in appropriate circumstances, as the "primary" employment given directly and indirectly by construction expenditures.[2]

The correct timing of controlled public works is a somewhat vexed question and one of major importance. The assumption usually made that they should be rapidly expanded as early as possible in a depression is open to question unless carefully qualified. For some process of readjustment is both inevitable and desirable once an unhealthy inflationary situation has been allowed to develop. Unless public works have previously been sufficiently retarded to prevent the development of serious maladjustments, the right time to launch an expanded program is not in the early stages of the depression but only after the strictly unavoidable amount of liquidation has been effected. When that point is reached, however, a stimulus may be needed to arrest a continued contraction of business brought about by the sheer cumulative momentum of the downward process. During depressions the volume of capital expenditures being made is not sufficient to balance the volume of monetary "saving". Expanded public works programs would go some way toward offsetting the decline in private construction outlays. The most effective way of stimulating revival is by accelerating the pace of new capital development. The increased purchasing power distributed in wages, salaries, the purchase of materials, and so forth, should generate increased activity by raising prices to a profitable level. As business recovers and private enterprise resumes capital outlays in normal volume, and prices and activity increase,

[2]See Kahn, R. F., "The Relation of Home Investment to Unemployment," *Economic Journal*, June, 1931; "Public Works and Inflation," *Journal of the American Statistical Association*, Supplement, March, 1933; Keynes, J. M., *The Means to Prosperity*, London, 1933, pp. 6-18.

public works programs would naturally have to be correspondingly contracted. The only circumstances in which enlarged public works expenditures might fail to have this effect and perhaps actually discourage private construction outlays is by creating alarm, a danger which should be remote if they represent part of a well-considered long-term policy.

It is not possible to decide in advance and *a priori* when the point at which public works programs could best be speeded is likely to be reached. The decision must in practice necessarily be difficult to make, and involves the danger of an incorrect reading of the current situation. The success of any action taken will in some degree be contingent upon the insight with which current data are interpreted and future tendencies forecast. The corresponding difficulty of knowing when, and to what extent, to retard public works on the upswing is of course equally great.

The case against public works in depressions collapses when it is asked at what other phase of the business cycle they could better be put in hand. The reasoning of those who oppose large expenditures at the trough of the cycle proves too much, inasmuch as it amounts to a case against *all* public works as such. Granting that governments must always be responsible for a certain volume of public construction—and this volume has in recent times been growing steadily, both absolutely and relatively to private construction, with the state's progressively enlarged economic activities—the onus rests upon the critics of public works in depressions of demonstrating not merely that there are certain dangers in their execution at such times, but of showing whether they could be better undertaken at some other period. It has been shown above that the best time is probably not in the early stages of the downswing. It is clearly absurd to argue that they should be undertaken during the boom phase of the cycle. If public works programs undertaken in depression tend to raise building costs and the cost of borrowing to the detriment of private enterprise, they are certainly not less likely to do so during the boom period. Instead, their effect would be further to intensify the inflation. Public construction is less likely to have the effect of raising building costs at the bottom of a depression, since private outlays have then fallen to a minimum. In the light of these considerations the conclusion is inescapable that public works should as far as possible be concentrated in periods of depression. The danger of incorrect timing, conceded in part above, cannot be evaded by a policy of inaction; it is inherent in the nature of government expenditures as such, and not only on public works.

The stimulation of business through the expansion of public works is in the last analysis an inflationary, or counter-deflationary measure, and the converse in periods of upswing. Under an international gold standard such a policy, it has already been shown, can be pursued by any one country only within narrow limits, short of concerted international action. This course adopted by a country in isolation must constitute a threat to its continued adherence to the gold base. This was precisely the difficulty throughout the present depression, till our abandonment of gold, with all proposals for vigorous expansion of construction programs, though many who recognized this danger did not regard it as a decisive objection. A policy of controlled public works, unless adopted internationally, is therefore at bottom inconsistent with the underlying principles of a freely automatic international standard based on gold, though not necessarily with a modified gold standard operated under central bank coöperation. On the other hand, under systems of irredeemable paper or otherwise "controlled" currencies, why should stimulated construction be necessary to effect credit expansion, and could not this end be pursued directly? The policy of flooding the banks with cheap money by means of a low rediscount rate supported by security purchases on a large scale may not, however, have the desired effect of creating bank deposits and increased consumer buying, or it may be long delayed. There is no guarantee that sound borrowers will come forward automatically. The course of action, though good, may not be sufficient in itself and may require other measures reinforcing it to get activity and prices rising. Past experience has repeatedly shown that making borrowing easier will not necessarily in a severe depression encourage business activity. That depends upon whether business men consider they can increase production profitably, and that, in turn, depends largely upon the trend of prices, it all being ultimately a question of profits, actual or prospective. The experience of recent months has been to the effect that deliberate measures increasing purchasing power may be necessary under a free paper standard if the rise in prices and the stimulation of activity is to be based on something more substantial than an ephemeral speculative movement likely to collapse again at any moment.

The objection has sometimes been advanced, however, that capital raised by public authorities for construction work in times of depression represents merely a diversion of resources from private industry to public enterprise, especially by heightening the cost of borrowing, and therefore cannot create any addition to the sum total of employment. It is further argued that the demand for construction materials and building labor resulting from increased public expenditures will, by raising building costs or preventing them from falling, increase the difficulties of private enterprise in the construction field. The argument rests, however, upon the fallacious assumption of a rigidly limited and inflexible volume of credit. Since there is usually during depression periods a surplus of idle funds seeking secure investment at attractive returns which private business is unable or unwilling to utilize in face of uncertainty, declining prices, and excess productive capacity, its use by public bodies need involve no transfer, inasmuch as the capital would otherwise not have been employed at all. Expansion itself provides the resources which make expansion possible: the funds needed to finance increased public construction outlays come partly from the reduced expenditures required for direct relief and partly by creating bank credits or preventing their continued contraction. And indeed the experience of governments has in general been that they could raise money in the capital market without increasing the difficulties of private enterprise. It should be emphasized, however, that a public works program undertaken in conjunction with an appropriate central bank policy can prove successful, especially under an international metallic monetary standard, only if government credit is secure, the capital market strong, and the demand for bonds elastic.

The further objection to public works expansion in depression, that the additional debt contracted involves a future increased burden of taxation, rests on a confusion of thought. Business recovery brings increased tax receipts without the imposition of additional taxation. Equally unfounded is the argument that public works expenditures financed by borrowing do injury in depressions by "unbalancing" the budget, for the answer is that the budget can be brought into an enduring balance only if the national income is increased, and this can come about only through a restoration of business activity. We cannot all grow prosperous if everyone, including the government, spends progressively less and less. That way lies universal impoverishment.

With regard to the charge of inevitable waste, no excessive waste need occur if projects have been planned ahead, but such as did would be insignificant in comparison with the economic wastage of idle and deteriorating man-power and capital equipment. Besides, since the unemployed have to be supported in any event out of public or private funds, the real net direct cost of public works, apart from their indirect stimulating effects, is much less than it seems, while in addition the community receives something in return for its expenditures. Thus the apparent magnitude of the cost is deceptive. For, first, there must be deducted from the gross cost both the saving in unemployment relief and the increased tax receipts which will in time flow into the treasury as a result of the increased incomes and profits of the recipients. Secondly, public outlays on capital developments bring the community a two-fold socially beneficial return, which relief expenditures do not: they augment its physical assets and they preserve the industrial skill and the morale of those given employment. Thirdly, as shown above, there are in addition their equally important indirect effects in creating "secondary" employment and in aiding recovery by starting the ball rolling again.

Finally, it is often asserted that a sufficient volume of genuinely needed public works cannot be found in depression periods to give substantial employment. This objection would of course fall to the ground if construction programs were to be planned ahead and retarded in periods of prosperity. But even though this was not the case during the present depression, still the statement was wholly unjustified, at least as regards the United States. For in all parts of the country billions of dollars worth of authorized and sometimes already initiated projects were suspended through the wholesale elimination of all possible construction items from numerous local budgets because of the shortage of funds, though this was not true of the Federal government. Road and bridge building, in particular, is an example of construction work suitable for this purpose both because it can be put in hand rapidly and entails expenditures which are bound to be made sooner or later. Schemes for slum-clearance and the erection of decent workers' dwellings suffer from the defect that hitherto in most cities comprehensive and detailed plans have not existed, but they offer almost boundless opportunities in the future for construction work of the highest social utility.

# VI. THE NATURE AND NECESSITY OF A PRICE SYSTEM

BY J. A. SCHUMPETER

I.

The reason why it may be useful to insert into our considerations a few remarks on the nature of price, highly theoretical though they may seem on the one hand and trivial though they may seem on the other, is simply that recent discussion on fundamental economic reform has shown that some people take the view, not new, of course, in itself, that prices and especially prices plus profits are nothing but an incident in the life of acquisitive society, that they are an obstacle to the full use of existing productive possibilities, and that they might with advantage be done away with. Prices have been compared to tolls levied for private profit or to barriers which, again for private profit, keep the potential stream of commodities from the masses who need them. The writer believes it to be a mistake to consider such views as beneath discussion and thereby to insure their survival. Among the theoretic tools needed in order to deal with this view are some of the oldest of our science, dating back to the seventeenth century and also some of the most recent ones which have been contributed to our theoretic arsenal only in the last few years. As the problems involved are familiar ground to economists, it will be possible to confine the following remarks to a few points, in fact little more than headings which could be worked out more fully.

The writer wishes to point out one thing at the outset: in the course of progress of economic analysis during the last twenty years or so, it has happened repeatedly that views largely held by practical men or amateurs which by-gone generations of economists have been in the habit of disposing of as simply foolish have, by newer methods, been shown to contain some element of truth after all, and sometimes quite a large one. In no case that the writer knows of has the reasoning itself which led to such views been rehabilitated. But whilst its errors remained what they were, newer methods of analysis have repeatedly shown by other reasoning that there was yet something to the proposition which the wrong reasoning ineffectually tried to prove. It would be easy to give instances. Our problem is among them, for though as much economic insight as can be got out of an elementary course on economics would seem to be sufficient to refute that view on prices, recent investigations on limited-competition and short-period phenomena have yielded results which will go a long way toward justifying in some measure the practical implications involved in that view.

2.

In order to show that price is a phenomenon incident to all forms of organization of society and to economic action in general, it is sufficient to look upon it as a coefficient of economic choice. That is to say, by paying a price for any commodity, buyers show a preference for that commodity as compared with other commodities which they could also buy if they wanted to, for the same money. At the point at which they stop buying, the price will exactly measure that preference for every one of them, and this is what is meant by calling price a coefficient of choice.

Now if we take the organization of a centralized social-ist state as an example of non-capitalist forms of society, it stands to reason that the central management would have nothing to go by in its decisions on the questions of the what and how of production unless it gave the comrades an opportunity to express their preferences with quantitative precision. This is equivalent to saying that the coefficient of choice of the members of such a society would have to be found out somehow, for instance, by assigning to them a certain number of claims to units of product in general and allowing them to express their preferences for the various commodities by means of those units. If then prices can be considered to be coefficients of choice, then the coefficients of choice of the comrades would be essentially prices. Moreover, in order to choose between the various possible methods of production, it would be necessary for the managers to attribute values to the means of production at their command which it would be possible to deduce from the coefficients of choice expressed by the comrades. These values would be essentially the same thing as the prices of the means of production in a capitalist organization.

The last sentence already shows that the phenomenon of price covers in fact the whole range of economic action. If a man produces whisky rather than bread from his rye, then what he does can be interpreted as bartering bread for whisky, and at the point at which he stops doing this we shall again be able to obtain a quantitative expression of his preferences and again get a coefficient of choice which in all respects is the same thing as price in a market. It is obvious that the choice between these two alternatives is not determined by technical considerations. It should be equally obvious that economic considerations of precisely the same kind enter into the choice of the method of producing either bread or whisky, and that it would be incorrect to say that the decision about the what of production is an economic matter and the rest, namely, the decision about the how of production, a technological matter. For whenever there is more than one way of producing a thing, and methods of production differ as to the relative quantities of the means of production they require, it will be necessary to take account of their relative scarcity, or to put it in another way, to consider how valuable the other products are which could also be produced by the individual units of the means of production which the producer contemplates using for a given purpose. These values of alternative production show themselves in capitalist society in the money price of the means of production and would show themselves in equivalent expressions in any other form of society. This explains why technically backward methods of production may still be the most rational ones provided the more perfect methods would require less of a plentiful factor and more of one which is less plentiful, and why the technically most perfect method of production is so often a failure in economic life. Hence rational production can never rest on exclusively technological considerations, at least not as long as all means of production are not at the command of a society in unlimited quantities. An economic dimension is, therefore, always necessary for the guidance of production, and this economic dimension at all times and under all circumstances finds expression in coefficients of choice which are fundamentally the same thing as prices in capitalist society. Of course, this does not mean that these coefficients would be numerically the same under all circumstances and in all forms of society, but they would always be of the same nature and fulfill the same purpose from which it follows that any attempt to do without them would be devoid of sense.

3.

Well-known arguments of very different degrees of scientific rigor have been put forward to show that a régime of perfect competition would invariably result in a maximum of welfare and also in a maximum of total product. The first proposition is wrong but the second is correct, or at least nearly so, provided we define competition as a state of things in which no buyer and no seller of any commodity or productive service is big enough to exert by his own action any influence on the price of the product he sells or the price of the means of production he buys. For this case it can also be shown, at least as a matter of broad practical probability, that the sources of waste inherent in such a society are smaller than those inherent in others, that the process of saving would not create disturbances and, incidentally, that if free competition prevailed absolutely unfettered *all over the world*, the gold standard, although not functioning ideally, would yet not be the cause of any great or violent disturbances. But the great scientific interest of all those and many other conclusions is for practical purposes very much reduced by the fact that competition in that sense not only does not exist but under modern conditions of large-scale production could not exist. It is here that the practical man and the amateur score. For it is not true that what can be proved for the case of perfect competition holds approximately for the case of imperfect competition, as the older theory uncritically assumed. On the contrary, it has been proved of late that in important respects imperfect or monopolistic competition will produce exactly the opposite of those results which might be expected from free competition in the theoretic sense. Without going into the matter I refer to the literature of the subject, especially to the new book by Edward Chamberlin entitled *The Theory of Monopolistic Competition*. As the man in the street never meant anything else by competition but the absence of agreements or interference from outside, and as he certainly visualized monopolistic competition when he talked about competition in general, he is perfectly right in attributing to it all sorts of waste as well as a systematic tendency to stop short not only of any technical but also of the economic optimum of quantity of product. We need only go on to insert into our picture various kinds of inertia and friction in order to realize that whatever gain in life-likeness we thereby attain is exactly proportional to the distance we travel from the assumptions of rationality and free competition. We may add that under the conditions of limited competition profits emerge of a kind unknown to the system of free competition and that, however wrong it may be to consider the fact of profits as such, as an obstacle to economic progress, and however true it may be that some kinds of profits have been the prime movers of progress actually achieved, yet the profits of limited competition are precisely of the kind of which the first of these two statements would be true. Of course, factual investigation and analysis of the results obtained would still be necessary before we could compare those wastes and lags of the system we have with those of every one of the alternatives, all of which have sources of waste and lags of their own.

The diagnostic value of the theory of free competition in the pure sense is, however, not impaired by these considerations. It is still worth while not only to work it out but to present it in a simplified form to the public because it shows where the sources of trouble do *not* lie and therefore by implication where we are to look for them. We may indeed sum up by pointing to the more important possibilities:

(1) It can be shown that the mere fact of turning coefficients of choice into prices by expressing them in units of money does not alter their nature or the way in which they function. But this has nothing to do with the question whether the monetary and credit mechanism which determines the unit of price-accounting harbors sources of disturbance or not.

(2) The proof that competitive equilibrium is stable does not admit of extension to the case of limited competi-

tion. And all deviations from an unrealizable ideal state of competition may be so many causes of instability and disturbance.

(3) Even a perfectly competitive state of things would be exceedingly sensitive to disturbance from outside. Such disturbances, which obviously are very plentiful at present, must primarily be looked to if we are to understand the instabilities and troubles of the day. Among them we must not forget to glance at the general humor of the social environment which, quite apart from specific measures resulting from it, may injure the efficiency of the capitalist machinery in a thousand subtle ways by its general hostility to the forms of life and methods of business with which capitalist society works.

# VII. MONETARY POLICY AND THE MONETARY STANDARD

BY ARTHUR D. GAYER

Under a freely automatic gold standard, whose essence consists in the subordination of domestic to international factors, control over internal movements of the price level must, as shown above in Special Report III, be narrowly circumscribed to conform to world movements. In contrast an autonomous currency, whether cut loose completely from gold, or attached to it only in some flexible manner, confers freedom of action in domestic monetary policy at some sacrifice of exchange stability. Pre-War, post-War and more recent experiences have alike conclusively demonstrated that prices can be raised under an autonomous standard, whatever the expediency of such a course and its after-effects, to almost any extent by currency and credit expansion. The examples of European post-War inflation can be passed over as too glaringly obvious to mention. But more recently Great Britain, Sweden, and the countries of the "sterling bloc" in general have convincingly demonstrated their ability, since they went off gold over two years ago, to keep their wholesale price levels not only stable, but much more so than those of the countries which continued on the gold standard, and at a level considerably above the latter. Whether price-level variations are primarily attributable to disturbances of the equation between the goods flow and the money flow originating on the latter, the monetary side, or on the former, the non-monetary side,—and much ink has been spilt in this controversy in argument at cross-purposes,—there remains a theoretical possibility of keeping prices relatively stable provided the monetary factor, namely the effective supply

of the means of payment, can be controlled. Even were it
to be granted that the monetary mechanism under the gold
standard is not primarily responsible for *generating* business
fluctuations, there would still remain the further question
whether it is not defective in preventing the occurrence
and mitigating the consequences of mistakes in the non-
monetary sphere. In light of these circumstances it is worth
considering whether a return by the United States and the
world at large to the full international gold standard at a
fixed invariable rate is desirable at all, and if so, what conditions are prerequisite for its restoration. It is not a sufficient defense of the full gold standard to point to the
various shortcomings to which alternative monetary systems are subject. The faults of the semi-automatic gold
standard itself cannot be ignored, but must rather be
recognized as the necessary price which has to be paid for
the enjoyment of its benefits.

Even under a free standard, which does not narrowly cir-
cumscribe any individual country's freedom of action as
does gold, it may not be easy in practice, and *a fortiori* it
may not be desirable, to correct fluctuations in the price
level by the application of monetary measures. There is
considerable variation in the degree of control possessed
by different central banks over their own monetary systems, and hence in their power to regulate the effective
supply of the total means of payment. The control of the
Bank of England over the creation of bank money and
credit is, for example, much more complete than that of
the Banque de France, the Reichsbank, or the Federal Reserve authorities, for different reasons in each case. Moreover, it is notoriously more difficult to stimulate recovery
from a depression through monetary action than to check
an incipient boom, for, as repeated experience has shown,
business may fail to respond in a bad depression to reduced
rediscount rates even when reinforced by appropriate open-

market operations. But all that this means is that, if the desired end of credit expansion and rising prices cannot be attained directly by traditional methods, recourse must be had to supplementary measures, such as enlarged public works programs or other government and quasi-public outlays which will increase expenditures and purchasing power, and thus stimulate both capital goods industries and the demand for consumer goods. The question is discussed more fully elsewhere (Special Reports V and VIII). Though it is true that, once maladjustments have been allowed to develop during a boom, some recession and readjustment are unavoidable, yet the aim of a policy of monetary control would be precisely to prevent the development of inflationary overexpansion. Furthermore, such readjustments as were found to be necessary would surely be much more easily effected under *relative* stability[1] of the price level than when there is superimposed upon them a drastic price deflation going far beyond the lengths required to effect these readjustments. There is a world of difference between a necessary measure of corrective liquidation involving some lowering of the general price level and the purely destructive price deflation produced by a panic-generated passion for liquidity accompanied by a wild international scramble for gold. It is one of the gravest defects of the gold standard, as hitherto operative, that it works by a process of overcompensation, alternately in one and

[1]The term stability, as used in this paper and in the other Special Reports by the author contained in this volume, should not be understood as being synonomous with a rigidly inflexible or "constant" price level. It should not be interpreted as necessarily excluding either *moderate* short-period movements in the price level or a *gradually* rising or falling secular trend, but is merely meant to denote the elimination of violent oscillations. If, thus employed, the term is admittedly unsatisfactory because open to misunderstanding, it is used for want of one which would better express our meaning. The question of the kind of movement in the price level which would be most desirable—and most easily attainable—for the preservation of a moving equilibrium in the cost-price structure, and the appropriate behavior on the part of non-monetary factors which would be required, is considered at length in the author's forthcoming study of Monetary Policy and Economic Stabilization.

then in the other direction, first allowing credit to be over-expanded and prices to rise excessively, and then enforcing as a corrective a disproportionately large measure of credit destruction and price deflation.

The argument so often advanced, as for instance by the Gold Delegation majority, that measures of credit expansion "may in some cases even lay the basis for a new expansion of credit which it may prove difficult to control,"[2] may be quickly disposed of. It amounts to taking the risk of starving the patient to death by refusing him food for fear that if allowed to eat he might kill himself by gluttony. Experience, especially post-War experience, has shown that inflation can be got in hand even at an advanced stage. Nor is it true, as demonstrated by the post-War stabilization of many much-inflated European currencies, that inflation must always of necessity be followed by a deflationary reaction. France, Italy, and Germany all experienced inflation without subsequent deflation. Only under the gold standard is inflation likely to be followed by deflation.

The disastrous consequences of instability in the standard of value need not be dwelt upon at length. Recent experiences in particular have made our realization of the evils of violent price fluctuations only too painfully keen. The confusion introduced into national economic life, and the cruel injuries and injustices inflicted on society by price chaos have often been described in detail. The evil has a twofold aspect. Rapid changes in the price level, by causing dislocation and disturbance throughout the whole price-cost structure, have a calamitous effect upon *productive activity;* but they also arbitrarily alter the *distribution,* as between different classes of society, of the national income which is the product of that economic activity. In addition they play havoc with smooth economic and con-

[2]*Final Report*, p. 47, para. 176.

sequently with political relations not only between classes but also between nations. A sharp fall in prices demands readjustments in the distribution of income and the structure of production of a drastic, far-reaching, and difficult kind throughout the whole price system, national and international.

The advocates of the traditional gold standard usually rest their case on a twofold ground: the superiority of an international over a local standard for the promotion of international economic relations; and the practical difficulties of preventing a paper or otherwise free system from passing out of control, whatever its ideal advantages in theory.

Differently expressed, the first count in this defense is that the full gold standard affords international commerce and finance the great boon of permanent stability in the foreign exchanges. Variations of rates are automatically restricted within the narrow limits of the gold points. The very real advantage of this convenience need not be stressed to a generation which has witnessed the hazards and uncertainties introduced by exchange fluctuations into foreign trade during post-War and more recent years of independent currencies. It is a twofold evil which impedes not only international trade but also international investment. For the former there is a partial remedy, for the latter none at all. Short of the development of an international system of free standards linked together under the leadership of one or two Great Powers, which might conceivably secure relative fixity of exchange rates, this advantage can be enjoyed only under an international gold standard. The risks introduced into short-term foreign trade transactions by fluctuating currencies can in some measure be eliminated or mitigated by the development of "forward exchange" markets. But the extent to which exchange risks can be avoided or reduced by recourse to these markets in the present stage of their development should not be exaggerated. They are as yet far from perfectly organized and tend to function best just when the need for them is least, namely in times of relative stability, and least adequately when their advantages would be greatest, in periods of wide fluctuation and uncertainty. In the course of time this weakness could probably be eliminated under an interconnected system of universally operative autonomous standards, and at least in more or less normal periods forward exchange markets could doubtless be organized in all the leading currencies and for varying maturities. The other difficulty, however, the impediment which fluctuating exchanges impose in the way of international lending, would still remain. Hedging on the forward exchange markets is not possible in this case. There is here no remedy at all. The risks of loss through exchange variations would be much increased, and would have to be borne by either borrower or lender. Were the full international gold standard permanently abandoned, one of the conditions which would have to be accepted would be a relative contraction, though by no means necessarily a complete cessation, of the volume of international investment. As argued below, this might not, especially for the United States, be too high a price to pay for the benefits of national autonomy in monetary policy. But the connection between exchange stability afforded by the gold standard and the very rapid development of both international trade and investment during the half century preceding the War was by no means accidental, and the process must have been markedly slower had not the gold standard afforded such good security against unforeseeable exchange risks. The development of an international monetary standard and of an international economy proceeded *pari passu*, and had inevitably so to proceed. Conversely the recent breakdown of the gold standard is in part attributable to its being, as we have seen, an international instrument in a world of growing economic nationalism.

The choice between stability of exchanges and stability of the internal price level must, when these ends prove incompatible, be influenced primarily by the relative importance of foreign trade and investment to the economic life of the country in question. For the United States, if it could be attained, internal stability would appear manifestly to be the more important in view of the overwhelmingly larger volume of transactions which are upset by internal as against foreign exchange instability. Indeed Keynes has argued that internal stability is to be preferred even in the case of a country whose foreign trade and overseas investments are of such vital importance to her as are Britain's.

The second part of the argument in support of the full gold standard amounts to a preference for placing the monetary system at the mercy of uncertain, unpredictable, and uncontrollable economic forces impinging from without, rather than intrusting the management of such a tremendously important factor for social good or evil to the frailty of human nature. It is not merely that the authorities charged with exercising these vast powers might be beset with the temptation to take the easiest course and lack courage to pursue the general public good in the face of pressure from powerful sectional interests, they might also often lack the knowledge and understanding to make wise decisions in complex, obscure, but highly important situations. The strength of the full gold standard is felt to lie in the greater freedom it enjoys from political pressure than any other standard. Against the danger of inflation gold does afford the security of an objective restraint upon the unlimited manufacture of a costless means of payment.

In periods of stress, however, the pressure required to maintain the gold standard may quite likely become an intolerably heavy burden. When that happens, the tendency is for the gold standard to be abandoned anyway, either unceremoniously or with pious expressions of pained regret. It is thus with much justice that critics charge it with being a fair-weather device. Indeed it is true that in the past the gold standard has tended to receive all the credit for the smooth functioning of industry, trade, and finance in times when it has been subjected to no unusual strain, while paper currencies have received the blame for the uncertainty and confusion of those periods of stress when, not being strong enough to weather them, the gold standard has broken down. The abuse of overissue which free currencies have experienced on spectacular occasions in the past, since it was inevitable in the circumstances, affords no evidence of inherent weakness in such standards. These experiences, however, though unjustifiably, have colored popular opinion with a prejudice against paper or otherwise "managed" currencies, despite the fact that the repeatedly made charge that there are no examples of a free standard which has not ultimately suffered severe depreciation, is, as shown below, emphatically not true. The memories of post-War inflation in Europe and of the Greenback era in the United States go far to explain the quite irrational preference for and sentimental attachment to gold as such in the minds of many individuals and whole nations, when the circumstances are quite different from those just mentioned and call for unprejudiced examination of the facts of the situation. It is natural that prudent people should hesitate to intrust the determination of the standard of value to treasury officials and central banking authorities in view of the ignorance and folly they have sometimes manifested in their past performances. But the possibilities of managed currencies cannot be fairly evaluated on the basis of experience with them when they have been adopted involuntarily under the stress of an acute crisis or emergency which has broken the gold standard. Furthermore, whether we like it or not, the monetary standard of the future, even if based on gold, is bound to be, as we have seen, an increasingly managed one under which the policy of central banks will as much determine as be determined by the value of gold.

The arguments in support of independent standards, being largely the reverse of the case for the gold standard, rest ultimately on an emphasis upon the paramount importance of securing relative stability in the internal cost-price structure even at some sacrifice of fixity of exchange parities. By allowing the foreign exchange value of a currency to be adjusted to the internal price and money income level instead of demanding an adjustment of the latter to the external gold level, an autonomous standard permits the value of the currency to be adjusted to a point at which domestic prices and costs are in equilibrium. It has been aptly remarked that "there is a logical conflict between the gold standard and domestic monetary stability".[3] Central banks not unreasonably feel it necessary to hold surplus reserves for protection against internal and external drains, but the gold standard assumes that banking systems are "loaned-up," that gold reserves are being fully utilized. Prior to the depression the Federal Reserve system was enabled, by virtue of its huge gold stocks, to flout the "rules of the game" by failing to allow these reserves to have their full influence upon the total volume of the means of payment, and to adapt its policy to the supposed internal needs of business. By doing so, it departed very far from the traditional and orthodox principles of the freely automatic gold standard and strayed into the realms of monetary management. After 1931, however, despite her large gold holdings, the policy of "reflation" was definite-

[3]Professor John H. Williams, "Monetary Stability and the Gold Standard", in *Gold and Monetary Stabilization* (Harris Foundation Lectures, 1932), pp. 152-3.  See also p. 148.

ly precluded so long as the United States was concerned about retaining the gold standard. For no matter how vast gold reserves may be, they can, in certain circumstances, be drained away in almost no time at all.

Prior to the depression the gold standard in the United States was already a managed standard, inasmuch as the value of gold was being artifically determined by central banking policy. Stabilization of the price level through rediscount policy is a course of action utterly at variance with the cardinal principle of the gold standard in its pre-War form of allowing gold movements to exercise their full effect on prices. It is unreasonable to require countries to let gold movements have their full influence on the price level to their own detriment in the interests of other countries, yet if they do not do so they violate the principles of the gold standard to the ultimate injury of all adherents to the system alike, themselves included. This dilemma between domestic and international needs did not, though it was present, cause serious difficulty prior to the war mainly because international finance and commerce were dominated by a single center. London's supremacy was undisputed, and to her course other countries had perforce to adapt their monetary policies whether it suited their internal conditions well or ill, so long as they wished to remain members of the international system and participate fully in its benefits. But these conditions no longer obtain.

Under the strict gold standard the internal control of prices is stultified by the necessity of maintaining stability of exchanges with other gold-standard countries. An expansive or restrictive credit policy independently instituted by any one country is visited by an excessive loss or gain of gold. Each gold-standard country must, by the same token, take part in these general credit movements and keep pace with the others, if it is not to suffer disturbances in its gold reserves. In fine, not only does the gold standard permit business fluctuations, it compels all countries which adhere to it to participate in them. In depressions this circumstance can easily produce violent destructive liquidation passing far beyond the limits required for the correction of maladjustments. An almost simultaneous competitive raising of bank rates by all gold-standard countries has very different results from the raising of its rate by any one of them singly for the purpose of counteracting a gold outflow. The international money flow is not thereby changed, but merely slowed down in general, and pressure is put upon internal business and international trade over the whole gold-standard area. The raising of the New York Federal Reserve rate in 1929 for the purpose of curbing stock exchange excesses was followed by a general raising of rates throughout the world and led to a competitive scramble for gold. The traditional gold standard is likely to work well enough in periods of "normal prosperity", but it permits and even encourages, as any fully international standard must do, the development of maladjustments on a world-wide scale by spreading the effects of excesses in either direction. In periods of crisis, particularly, it tends, before it breaks, to reinforce rather than alleviate depression.

These observations indicate that the heart of the monetary problem lies in the clash between internal and international requirements. The narrow issue of possible conflict between a policy of domestic stabilization and one of foreign exchange stability raises the much broader question of the choice between using the monetary mechanism to serve the needs of the nation's internal economic development and of keeping it responsive to the sometimes exacting demands of the international situation. We are not entitled to assume that these two ends must always be in harmony. On the contrary, there is nothing in the nature of things which could lead us to expect that they should be. Fixed exchange parity, which gives room for free play only within the narrow limits of the gold points, demands that all readjustments should be made *internally* by each member of the gold standard system through pressure brought to bear upon a flexible domestic structure. This burden of readjustment may, however, as we have seen, be imposed upon an economic system which lacks sufficient elasticity to allow it to be adapted to the framework of the international system save with the most painful difficulty. This is not a fault of the gold standard as it has hitherto functioned, or even of the gold standard as such. A reformed full gold standard, managed under central bank coöperation, or even a truly international paper system, one which laid emphasis on international economic integration, would encounter the same dilemma to some extent and have in large part the same defect, though satisfactory compromise could probably be reached more easily in this case. The question is thus not the narrow one of when, and on what conditions, or even whether we should return to gold, but the broader one of whether it is advisable to return to a fully international standard at all.

All countries would benefit from *relative* stability in their internal price levels, but the form and conditions of stability are by no means likely to be identical in all cases. Different countries enjoy on the one hand divergent rates of economic development, and, on the other, varying degrees of flexibility in their cost structures. In addition they differ widely in respect to a great many other economic factors—the relative importance of their foreign trade, their debtor or creditor position on balance, the division of national activity between agriculture and manufacturing, and so forth. The kind of movement in the price level which satisfactorily meets the needs of one country may not be well adapted to the needs of others. Thus a country which is undergoing rapid development as a result of technical improvements which produce unit cost reductions is likely to be most benefited in the long run by a slowly falling price level, unless wages and other costs are also raised correspondingly rapidly. Otherwise the excessive profits which will result must produce over-expansion, maladjustment, and eventual reaction. The economic development of other countries, however, which will be proceeding largely independently, may be quite different. They may be advancing at a slower rate, or stagnating, or even conceivably retrogressing. Again, varying degrees of flexibility in their economic structures may render wage readjustments relatively easy or highly difficult to effect. In consequence their positions may be such for one reason or another that their needs will be best served by a fairly constant price level, or by one which declines only very slowly, or perhaps even by one which rises gently.

These hypothetical reflections find a wealth of concrete illustration in the world's economic development during the post-War decade. It should be sufficient, however, to mention one example, the contrast between the situations in this respect of the United States and Great Britain. As implied just above, the best price level for the United States during the period of rapid mechanization and consequently falling real costs from 1925 to 1929 would, in view of the failure of wages to rise correspondingly fast, have been one which fell more rapidly than it actually did, so that inflated profits might have been prevented. During these same years Great Britain's wholesale price index moved down slowly in step with America's, but in doing so imposed a great strain upon her economic life. In contrast to the United States her needs would have been best served, in view of her less rapid technical advance coupled with the rigidity of her wage rates, by a price level which fell *less rapidly* than it actually did, or by one which remained constant, or even perhaps which rose slowly. Moreover, an international monetary standard which imposes uniformity upon all its adherents irrespective of individual differences in their circumstances, visits the sins of one upon the others in spreading deflation from a country where it is needed for the correction of capital overexpansion to others where inflationary overdevelopment has not occurred and which therefore do not require deflation.

It is partly because of the uniformity which the gold standard imposes despite divergent rates of economic development that so many countries have had recourse in increasing degree to the expedient of trade barriers and similar restrictions in order to secure that measure of domestic freedom which they find imperative for their national economic needs but which is denied them by participation in an international system. In the exigencies of the gold standard itself are to be found to some extent the origin and explanation of the post-War tendency toward economic "autarchy." Thus the international gold standard, which at once has for its rationale the facilitation of world economic intercourse and demands for its successful operation a large degree of freedom in international trade, paradoxically encourages the erection of obstructions to the free flow of goods and often does almost as much indirectly to hinder as it does directly to promote the volume of world trade. That this statement is no exaggeration is vividly shown by the amazing and self-contradictory spectacle presented today of nations imposing exchange and other restrictions on international trade to protect the external values of their currencies, when the whole purpose of exchange stability is the promotion of international trade and investment.[4]

[4]The following recently expressed opinion is of great interest as coming from a Director of the Bank of England and a former Treasury official of distinguished practical experience in international financial affairs: "In sacrificing stability of internal prices to stability of the external exchanges and in ignoring the economic and financial independence of the units of which the world is made up, the attempt to treat it as a financial unit

These considerations do not constitute a conclusive case against an international standard in view of the many advantages it has been shown to possess in other directions. They do show, however, that its merits are counterbalanced by defects of a very serious order. To point out these shortcomings does not amount to a plea for "economic nationalism", but is rather a frank recognition of the frequent divergence of the needs of different nations. The dilemma of an international standard is the necessity of simultaneously preserving the benefits of exchange stability between the various countries adhering to it and insuring them individually sufficient local autonomy in their internal credit policies. If these two ends cannot be satisfactorily reconciled, there remains the possibility that something short of a fully international monetary standard may perhaps be found in the future most suitable to a world which is as yet neither internationally united nor internationally homogeneous.

Though it is true that short-term fluctuations of economic activity have no direct connection with variations in the supply of gold, being characterized by alternate expansion and contraction of the total effective supply of the means of payment, business cycles are profoundly affected by the international gold standard in three important respects. Whether the business cycle is regarded primarily

---

capable of using to advantage a single monetary standard has been the direct cause of economic friction between the nations. 'This high man, aiming at a million, misses an unit.' For the gold standard yokes together in an uncomfortable partnership individual economic units of which the pace and direction of development are dissimilar and divergent. Just because they feel themselves hampered by the financial tie, the nations are driven, in defence of their right to decide the course of their own national life, to adopt economic expedients, such as high protective tariffs, prohibitions, currency and exchange restrictions, transfer moratoria, and such like, which play havoc with all forms of international intercourse. With their prices tied to the chariot wheels of gold, stability in their internal trading and productive activities is beyond their reach, and the absence of assured stability at home makes them set up barriers against the external world and minimizes the extent of the contributions they can make to world interchanges." (Sir Basil Blackett, *Planned Money*, 1933, p. 179.)

as a monetary phenomenon or not, there can be no question that control exercised to mitigate its severity must, short of international action, be narrowly restricted under the international gold standard in the subordination of internal monetary policy to the exigencies of world movements. The violence of business fluctuations tends in consequence, as we have seen, to be aggravated by the cumulative effect of interdependent forces operating in the same direction. This process is likely to be especially marked in times of unusual tension, when the shortcomings of the gold standard are seen in their clearest light. For at such moments the desperate anxiety of central banks each to protect the metallic base of its own currency is liable to produce a feverish and senseless scramble for gold. This may impose terrific deflationary pressure on the price level and business activity to the extent even of causing a veritable panic which can only end in countries with less ample reserves or less flexible price structures being overwhelmed by the storm and being forced off gold.

Apart, however, from its effects in precluding any serious attempts to mitigate cyclical fluctuations and in intensifying panics through purely destructive price deflation, the working of the international gold standard influences not only the amplitude of the business cycle as such, but the relative duration of the different phases composing it. The effect of variations in gold supplies, relatively to the monetary demand for gold, upon the secular trend of prices is not open to question. The historical data assembled by Professors W. L. Thorp and W. C. Mitchell demonstrate in the clearest manner that the relative duration of periods of prosperity and depression is directly attributable to the direction of the secular trend of the wholesale price level, as shown by the following table.[5]

[5]Mitchell, W. C., *Business Cycles* (National Bureau of Economic Research), p. 411.

| PERIOD | SECULAR TREND OF PRICES | YEARS OF PROSPERITY PER YEAR OF DEPRESSION |
|---|---|---|
| U. S. A. | | |
| 1790–1815................... | Prices rising | 2.6 |
| 1815–1849................... | Prices falling | 0.8 |
| 1849–1865................... | Prices rising | 2.9 |
| 1865–1896................... | Prices falling | 0.9 |
| 1896–1920................... | Prices rising | 3.1 |
| ENGLAND | | |
| 1790–1815................... | Prices rising | 1.0 |
| 1815–1849................... | Prices falling | 0.9 |
| 1849–1873................... | Prices rising | 3.3 |
| 1873–1896................... | Prices falling | 0.4 |
| 1896–1920................... | Prices rising | 2.7 |

In periods of rising price trends the peak of each business cycle is likely to be higher than that of the preceding one; the phase of expanding activity and rising prices is thus likely to be of relatively prolonged duration, and the cyclical fall to be correspondingly mild. With an upward trend of prices the depression period of the cycle is minimized and severe panics are less likely to occur. In periods of declining price trends, on the other hand, the depression phase of the cycle is accentuated, and the expansive phase relatively short-lived. Crises especially are liable to manifest great violence, and the recovery from them to be slow, because sufficiently severe liquidation must be effected to bring prices down to a new permanently low level.

Apart from cyclical fluctuations, it is true that in the nineteenth century the gold standard was successful in affording reasonable stability of prices over relatively long periods of time. Between 1826 and 1914 the price index in Great Britain fluctuated only between 70 and 130, a variation which is very moderate compared with its movements during the much shorter period since 1914. Yet there were great changes in both the world supply of and the demand for monetary gold during the century preceding the War. The resultant relative secular stability of prices was not wholly fortuitous, because the search for new sources of gold and new methods of exploitation is likely to be prosecuted with especial vigor during periods of relative scarcity. Yet a large element of sheer chance remains in the adequacy of the volume of the gold supply which will be forthcoming at any given time in response to increased demand. There are no scientific grounds for the belief that a gold shortage will always be automatically rectified, and that the supply of gold will roughly keep step with the demand for it.

No reasonable advocacy of a return to gold can take the form of proposing that we simply restore the gold standard as it existed prior to the depression, without remedying the various defects which have been revealed in it as being responsible for its breakdown. What, then, are the minimum conditions under which a return to a full international gold standard might be considered? The necessary requirements are briefly as follows:[6]

(1) The first and most obvious condition is a satisfactory settlement of the war debts and reparations question, preferably by virtual cancellation, to remove this mischievous factor from interference with the normal current of international trade. Readjustment in certain cases of private debts to prevent defaults will also be necessary.

(2) Second is the reëstablishment of a reasonable degree of freedom in the international flow of goods and services by the removal of the more obnoxious forms of trade

[6]This Special Report was written before the recent monetary legislation under which the dollar has been revalued. Since these measures, however, permit the government to vary the gold content of the dollar, as it deems advisable, within a twenty per cent margin, they are in substantial harmony with the proposals made in the text below and can hardly be regarded as constituting a return to the full international gold standard in the strict sense. Though now based loosely on gold, the monetary standard of the United States still remains, potentially at least, a relatively autonomous one.

barriers, conspicuously exchange restrictions and the like. It should be recognized, however, that the reduction of import duties, quotas, and so forth, is likely to be a slow and uncertain process, conflicting in many cases with policies dictated by internal needs. Our Industrial Recovery Act and Agricultural Adjustment Program may be cited in this connection. A certain measure of control over the foreign trade of the country in the interests of long-range national plans will make essential the retention of certain trade restrictions.

(3) Third is a general and sufficiently specific undertaking by central banks that in the future management of the gold standard "the rules of the game" will be better observed than in the past, and particularly that gold movements will be permitted to exercise their full influence on the price levels of the countries both losing and receiving gold.

This undertaking, however, would have to be coupled with another measure of coöperation between central banks providing for common policies in the joint management of the gold standard to preserve reasonable stability in the value of gold. Our return to the full gold standard on any other terms would be highly hazardous and might prove most unfortunate. To put this condition into effect, agreement will be required among the Great Powers that such economies in the use of gold will be practised as will prevent a rise in its value. The prevention of future gold shortage may quite well require that the stipulations regarding legal reserves now in force be drastically modified or possibly even entirely abolished.

(4) But none of these measures can accomplish much without a previous restoration of more normal activity and employment. A general rise in the world level of wholesale commodity prices and the restoration of equilibrium between prices, wages, and debt charges must first be effected

before a return to an unqualified gold standard at a fixed invariable rate can be safely considered.

(5) In addition to international action along the above
lines certain internal reforms on the part of individual
countries will also be indispensable. Each of these must
therefore make sure that its internal economic structure
possesses sufficient flexibility to permit its adherence to an
international system with prospect of success. However improved, a truly international monetary standard cannot
hope to function well without such a condition being fulfilled.

(6) Greater flexibility of many internal factors will be
required to insure the successful functioning of the gold
standard, but in some respects *less* freedom will be necessary. In particular, much more control than hitherto must
be exercised over the volume of foreign lending to see that
it is brought into harmony with the amount of the foreign
balance. There are no grounds for the widespread but naïve
belief that these two forces must of necessity be automatically equated.

The resumption of the full gold standard is desirable only
if these guarantees are secured for its good behavior in the
future. They will admittedly require the practice of much
more continuous coöperation among central banks of issue
than seems likely at the moment to be forthcoming, but a
return to gold in the strict sense on any other conditions
would involve a cost heavier than the probable benefits.
The wisest course would then be to concentrate on internal
stabilization under an autonomous standard, either cut
loose from gold or attached to it under some elastic arrangement. The dangers of a premature return to the full
gold standard, if fresh difficulties in the future are to be
avoided, are pointedly illustrated by England's post-War
experience.

If it is felt that the advantages of an international standard outweigh its defects, then probably a reformed gold standard, operated under the conditions indicated above, granted they can be put into effect, will for some time to come be the best choice, in view of the impossibility likely to be encountered of securing the necessary agreement on any alternative international standard entirely cut loose from gold. The choice which lies before us, however, is not one between a managed and an automatic system. Whatever standard is adopted, whether a local or an international one, will require a great deal of management. The emphasis in one case will be laid on internal control, in the other on international management. Even the Gold Delegation majority, who showed themselves unsympathetic in general to the idea of monetary management, recognized that management through international coöperation will be needed to make a rehabilitated international gold standard function adequately in the future.

The statement has often been made that currencies divorced from gold have always come to grief in the past and suffered damaging depreciation through excessive over-issue. Spectacular instances of unrestrained inflation, especially during post-War years, are usually cited as evidence. But the fallacy of the notion that free standards must necessarily get out of control can easily be exposed. It is supported by neither American nor English experience. No wild inflation has occurred under paper money in this country since the Revolutionary War. Even during the Civil War, in 1864, when the price level in England under the gold standard stood at 127, it was 193 in the United States (base, 1910–14 = 100). The worst periods of inflation in the United States since the Revolutionary War have occurred *under the gold standard:* in 1920, when wholesale prices stood at 226 (base as above), and during the stock market boom of 1928–29. During the periods when England has been off gold, from 1797 to 1821, from 1914 to

1925, and again since 1931, 37 years in all out of 137, the currency was never abused by inflationary excesses.

It is strange that the statement that free currencies are uncontrollable should still be made by monetary authorities in the light of the experience with them during the last few years, a period of acute economic pressure. For paper currencies showed themselves far more stable than gold currencies between 1931 and 1933, despite the critical difficulties of the times and the grave temptations they offered to governments to indulge in inflationary finance. During these years it was not the pound sterling, the Canadian dollar, the Scandinavian currencies, and so forth, which were unstable, but the American dollar, the franc, the mark, and other gold currencies. The paper moneys of the "sterling area" retained a remarkably steady purchasing power on the whole, while gold underwent an outrageous appreciation in value. The percentage change in the wholesale commodity price level was as follows in various countries respectively on and off gold between September, 1931, when England left the standard, and March, 1933, when we did so:[7]

| GOLD STANDARD COUNTRIES | | PAPER STANDARD COUNTRIES | |
|---|---|---|---|
| U. S. A. | —15.5 | England | —1 |
| France | —18 | Sweden | —2 |
| Netherlands | —21 | Canada | —9 |
| Germany | —17 | Australia | —4 |
| Italy | —12 | Japan | +18 |

On the whole, if there has been excess in the management of the free currencies, it has been an excess of prudence and caution; they have been operated almost as if they were gold currencies and the freedom of action given by severance from the gold base has been used seemingly only to prevent further disastrous deflation, and not, except in the case of the United States at the present time,

[7]Federal Reserve Bulletin; figures for Sweden and Australia from Statistical Year Book of the League of Nations, 1932–33.

to put into effect a positive policy of reflation. If free currencies can be managed with such conspicuous success in affording stability of prices in times of acute stress, how much better are the prospects of successful control in more normal periods? Great Britain and the countries which followed her off gold in 1931 were spared the long and agonizing process of devastating deflation to which the United States was subjected during the next eighteen months by her desperate attempt to cling to gold at all costs. The cost was too high, and incurred with less excuse than in the case of other gold standard countries. America in clinging to gold precluded every course of action for the deliberate encouragement of business recovery, largely, it would appear, through sheer timidity. In the end, the attempt to preserve the gold standard, after it had come near wrecking the entire economic life of the nation, issued in failure, and the United States found it necessary to abandon gold after all. The great sacrifice made to retain it was made in vain.

The reason why paper currencies have often depreciated badly in the past has not been, except in the most superficial sense, the abandonment of gold, but force of circumstances. The ultimate cause of inflation is the emergency, whether war, political crisis, or economic collapse, which compels resort to inflationary finance and cannot be weathered otherwise, and so breaks the gold standard. Wild inflations are always due to government bankruptcy, as during the American, the French, the German, and the Russian revolutions alike. Under such conditions it is hardly surprising that moderation of issue is not practiced, since gold is abandoned precisely for the purpose of obtaining relief from the intolerable financial strain imposed by the emergency. Once the latter has been weathered, experience has shown that the currency usually undergoes no further depreciation. Thus the gold standard is no real protection against inflation: when conditions make imperative the resort to inflation, or to counter-deflationary measures, the gold base is abandoned. In times of serious crisis it proves a failure because the attempt to put the currency system in a straight-jacket is bound to break down.

Furthermore, the inflation which has occurred under paper money has often proved less destructive and inflicted less injury than the deflation which the exigencies of the gold standard have on occasions imposed. German post-War inflation eventually ended in complete monetary chaos, but the inflation of the French and Belgian francs, the Italian lira, and other falling currencies enabled their respective countries to avoid the worst of the post-War depression. On the other hand, whatever the complete explanation of England's prolonged and continuous industrial stagnation during the decade following the War, there can be no doubt that the deflationary pressure required by the policy of financial purism in putting her back on gold at the pre-War parity was a serious contributing factor.

The primary immediate desideratum in the matter of monetary policy for the United States and the world at large is a price level which rises gradually for some time to come, provided it is associated with general confidence in the price-raising methods or impulses. This does not mean that a rise in the prices of all commodities and services would be desirable, or that the degree of rise in all cases should be the same. On the contrary a reduction of certain prices would be highly beneficial, while as regards the others it is in general the most depressed which stand most in need of increase. Apart, however, from a rise in the *general* level of prices for a time there is little hope of increasing production and trade or of correcting the still paralyzing disparity between debts and income. The absorption of the vast mass of unemployed and the redemption of many industries, including the great basic industry of agriculture, are impossible apart from the stimulation of business which is reflected in rising prices.

It should be clearly realized, however, that rising prices are not an end in themselves. Only in so far as it accompanies and results from increased activity, and facilitates the reëstablishment of a profit margin between cost factors and selling prices, is a rise in the general level of prices desirable. To argue otherwise is to place the cart before the horse. Profits cannot emerge as long as prices continue to fall faster than costs, but they likewise cannot emerge if costs increase more rapidly than prices, or if the rise in prices is based on nothing more substantial than an ephemeral speculative movement or is otherwise artificially engineered and unaccompanied by an increase in effective purchasing power. We cannot enter here into the examination of the best methods of accomplishing the desired objective of increased business activity accompanied by rising prices. They are discussed elsewhere in this volume. On the whole the direct methods of monetary manipulation for increasing the total volume of the means of payment, though they may be efficacious when resorted to in moderate measure and under careful guidance, need to be supplemented and reinforced by indirect methods, such as large and well-timed programs of public works, discussed above in Special Report V. For the direct methods—greenback issues, dollar devaluation, gold purchases, even low Federal Reserve rediscount rates supported by large-scale security purchases—all possess in varying degree the serious limitation that though they may increase the potential supply of money, they do not, simply of themselves, increase the demand for it. Something more than making borrowing easy or money cheap is required to create bank deposits, stimulate investment, and encourage business activity. Effective measures are needed to increase purchasing power and the demand for producers' goods if the rise in prices is to be well founded.

Granting that a rise in prices, subject to the conditions just mentioned, would be beneficial, how great a rise is desirable? The frequent suggestion that the 1926 or 1929 price level should if possible be restored is more than dubious. Since the recession much drastic readjustment has taken place both through the scaling down of the debt structure and through wage and salary reductions. If the 1926 or 1929 price level were restored these factors would also have to be readjusted upwards again. There is also reason for believing that the 1929 price level was too high in the United States because, as a result of unit cost reductions, it fostered the boom by creating excessive profits. Moreover, since 1929 further cost reductions, effected through improvements in productive technique as well as through reductions in monetary wages, have continued rapidly, as in most previous depressions. No definite figure can be prescribed in advance as the goal at which to aim. This will depend on a complex of factors, prominent among them the relative movements of wages and profits, which in the United States are at the moment quite incalculable. The criterion will be a balanced condition of full normal employment and activity, with costs and receipts in a relation which makes economic enterprise profitable but not excessively so. Needless to say, the actual decision will in practice be difficult to make and will demand the exercise of much judgment. Furthermore, though the ideal level would be the one which effects the best mutual adjustment between debts, wages, freight and utility rates, and other costs, it may be advisable to accept a compromise between this level and a practical one set by considerations of expediency on account of the dangers of prolonged disturbance of credit and investment conditions.

Turning from immediate to permanent desiderata in the matter of monetary policy, the primary need is for a monetary system which will insure *relative* stability in the price level. Again, this objective is to be sought not as an end in itself but as a means toward, and only to the extent that it is compatible with, the preservation of a moving equilibrium in the cost-price structure. We may for the moment leave open the question, as answerable only in the light of the behavior of non-monetary factors, whether a *slow* secular trend of prices in one or other direction may not be preferable to an *absolutely* stationary level. There should be no difference of opinion, however, that if the economic order we know is to survive in any form at all, the series of violent price movements which the world has witnessed since the War must be prevented in the future. Of secondary importance as a goal of monetary policy, though one well worth striving for in so far as it is consistent with the main desideratum, is some such stability in foreign exchange as the international gold standard assured in its traditional form.

The concomitant non-monetary conditions necessary to insure the preservation of economic balance under a monetary policy whose aim was relative stability of the price level could never, however, be lost sight of with impunity. Even when reinforced by means of a flexible system of public capital outlays and other measures for varying the volume of purchasing power actually put into circulation, a policy of central bank control may not in itself prove powerful enough to produce a moving economic stability unless the right balance is preserved between various classes of prices and incomes, and especially between the relative rates of saving and investment. For the purpose of securing this proper internal relation between different prices and incomes, specific industrial controls may well be required in addition to general monetary measures: devices for regulating prices and supplies in particular markets and relative to one another; for keeping wages and profits in correct relation; for maintaining equality between net foreign lending and the net foreign balance, and so forth.

As emphasized above, the pursuit of price stability does not mean that the objective should be a rigidly constant price level moving along neither a moderately upward nor downward trend; or that an attempt should be made to eliminate all cyclical movements whatsoever; or certainly that banking policy should be regulated solely with an eye to the wholesale commodity price index and be blind to all other criteria. The belief that price stabilization can in itself be identified with a dynamic economic stability is a naïve fallacy, though it is difficult to see how the latter objective can be attained unless the former is first assured. The entire economic system cannot be controlled by operating a single lever, or through the monetary mechanism alone, but control of that lever is indispensable in the pursuit of balanced economic advance. Under a monetary policy the aim of which was stability of prices, the closest and most careful attention would have to be given to the movements and interactions of a large variety of other factors, monetary and non-monetary alike. Experience prior to 1929 clearly demonstrated that violent maladjustments can develop under a stable commodity price level if the behavior of non-monetary factors is not appropriate to such a price level.[8] The ultimate criterion in a system of private enterprise, under which activity is pivoted on profits, must be the movements of the profits index. If unit costs are being steadily reduced as a result of improvements in productive technique or organization, the preservation of economic stability requires either that prices be reduced or that monetary wages be raised proportionately. Otherwise

[8]The problem is discussed at length in Chapter 6 of the author's forthcoming study of Monetary Policy and Economic Stabilization.

excessive profits will accrue to entrepreneurs and induce capital overexpansion and security inflation which must inevitably result in a reaction that monetary policy is powerless to prevent. For the economic system to function well, profit margins must be adequate but not excessive. Since a price level which falls in proportion to unit cost reductions due to increased economic efficiency and thus passes on the increased product of industry to consumers in the form of an enhanced purchasing power of their incomes is not only extremely difficult to secure under the very imperfectly competitive conditions of today, but is also undesirable on other practical and psychological grounds, as for instance from the point of view of labor, it is preferable that the objective of monetary policy should, if possible, be a relatively stationary price level. But this preference is conditional upon the steady distribution, in rising wages and salaries, of the progressive increase in national income which may be expected in an advancing economy. Proposals to this end are made elsewhere in this volume. Such a policy of price stabilization thus implies very much more than an attempt to regulate economic activity through monetary control alone. The monetary authorities could never for a moment be indifferent to the behavior of a variety of other, non-monetary, elements. The total picture would have to be kept continuously in mind and unremitting attention given not only to actual price movements but also to the volume of production, the condition of employment, the movement of wage rates and payrolls, the rate of business earnings, the yield on various types of investment, the volume of new security issues, the demand for credit, the volume of foreign trade and foreign lending, and so forth. Thus though the *aim* of monetary policy would be to keep commodity prices relatively stable, the criteria for assessment and for action would be manifold, and the purpose, and test of success, of the policy would be the preservation of a proper balance between the various elements in the internal cost-price structure. In the last analysis the consideration of paramount importance is the maintenance within that structure of the right relationship between cost factors and selling prices, one which prevents prices from rising too much above costs or costs from cutting too deeply into profits. There is no especial virtue in any particular price level in itself and for its own sake. The best price level will be the one which best facilitates that mutual adjustment of costs and prices, promptly and with least friction, which is continually necessary in a progressive economy.

The stabilization we seek must thus be subject to the condition that we live in a dynamic, progressive economy. It is sometimes argued that because in such an economy the rate of interest which would keep prices stable is different from the rate needed to preserve that equilibrium between saving, investment and consumption which should be the ultimate objective of monetary policy, therefore the pursuit of absolute price stability must end in failure by permitting maladjustments to develop between these factors. If a counsel of perfection is sought, this argument is valid, but whatever monetary policy is adopted will create some difficulties in an economically advancing community, for that is the price of progress. But if perfection is unattainable we need not on that account relapse into despair and abandon all attempt to reach reasonable economic stability through a policy of price stabilization coupled with and reinforced by appropriate controls over non-monetary factors. A habitable middle ground remains between absolute stability and the complete instability of the past. Thus the objective of monetary policy should be not the elimination of all fluctuation whatsoever in prices, but a price level which varies within moderate limits, and which, while preventing violent and catastrophic alternations of business activity between boom and depression, permits a mild and healthy up and down movement. If such a policy were reinforced by devices which evoked or produced the appropriate response in wage levels, no serious disequilibrium leading to maladjustments need develop between saving and investment, and the cyclical variations which business experienced would be moderate, tolerable, and on the whole beneficial. Reasonable price and economic stability both in the short and long run would be secured and the disastrous alternations would be eliminated which threaten to destroy the entire social structure.

The foregoing discussion should have made it clear that it is not possible at the moment of writing to lay down, dogmatically and apart from the concrete circumstances of the situation as it develops, the lines which American monetary policy should follow in the future. Much will depend not only on the course of economic events but also upon the monetary aims and policies of other countries and their willingness to coöperate with us. In summarizing our conclusions, the alternatives may be briefly presented.

(1) A hasty and premature return to the full international gold standard system should be avoided. The technical problems alone which would first have to be solved are so complex and difficult that should a restoration of a full gold standard along traditional lines be effected eventually, it would of necessity have to follow a preliminary period of experimental *de facto* stabilization. Past experience has almost invariably shown this to be a necessity. But even granting the satisfactory solution of technical problems, a return to the full gold standard should be contemplated only when there are good prospects that it can be so reconstructed that its future behavior will be an improvement on its past performance. The prerequisite conditions have been pointed out above. If a sufficient degree of international coöperation can be secured

between central banks to insure these conditions, chief among which is that the gold standard will be so managed in the future as to secure a reasonable stability of world prices, then adoption of this much modified and improved gold standard would probably be advisable.

(2) Such an internationally managed gold standard would be preferable to a number of independent paper systems. In view of the difficulties, however, of attaining this end, a transitional system might be possible through the coöperative action of the United States and Great Britain. A firm understanding between these two countries so to control gold as to keep its value stable would amount to something not far removed from stabilization of the world's gold price level. It would also insure stability of exchanges not merely between the dollar and sterling, but over virtually half the world, since it would include the countries with currencies linked respectively to these units.

(3) The establishment of a satisfactory international monetary system over this dollar-sterling area with the double objective of internal price and exchange stability, is not, however, dependent upon a return to the full gold standard at an invariable rate. If a restoration of a gold standard along the lines sketched above proves impossible of attainment, the United States would be, owing to the vastly greater importance of her internal over her external trade, in a peculiarly fortunate position for the adoption, should it prove desirable, of an autonomous currency system divorced from gold or attached to it in some flexible manner. If she did adopt a managed currency, she need not be doomed to find herself financially isolated. If agreement with Great Britain could be reached that she too would put into force the policy of regulating her currency to keep its internal purchasing power stable, variations in the exchange rates between these two powers, together with their financial satellites, could be restricted for the most

part within a fairly narrow range without great difficulty through the operation of exchange equalization funds and other devices. The means would have been found for reconciling internal price stability with the interests of international trade, without much surrender of national freedom to the demands of an internationally managed system. As to relations with those countries which might still remain linked to gold at a fixed invariable rate, if buying and selling prices for gold were fixed and maintained unaltered for considerable periods of time, excessive short-period fluctuations of the exchanges would be eliminated. The currencies of the countries which participated in this system would not be linked to one another at a definite, permanently unchangeable rate of exchange; relatively stable exchanges would be rather the natural consequence of the maintenance by each of stability in its own domestic price level. If such a scheme admittedly falls somewhat short of perfection in failing to provide a worldwide monetary standard giving both price stability and complete permanent exchange fixity, at least it represents a first long step in that direction and offers a program which, in present circumstances, has better prospects of realization. It is one, moreover, which the United States can give the world a lead in putting into effect. Under such a system the objectives of monetary policy would be twofold. *Externally*, the objective would be to secure as much agreement as possible with other nations for the relative stabilization of exchanges as far as this was compatible with internal monetary aims. *Internally*, it would be the preservation, in so far as the monetary mechanism can contribute to this end, of a moving equilibrium in the cost-price structure.

# VIII. THE FLOW OF PURCHASING POWER

## BY ALVIN H. HANSEN

The stream of income which functions as purchasing power in the market is, under our money and credit economy, subject to violent fluctuations. In boom times the income stream is augmented beyond what is justified by the productive process: (1) by the creation of an excessive volume of bank credit, (2) by intensive utilization of existing bank credit, and, sometimes, (3) by the disgorging of previous hoardings of cash. In times of depression the income stream is drained off (1) by diverting some part of it into the extinguishment of indebtedness to banks, (2) by a less intensive utilization of deposits (credit hoarding[1]), and, at times, (3) by actual cash hoarding.

The hoarding and dishoarding of money and credit, the extinguishment and creation of bank credit, are all alike the results of innumerable individual decisions. It is the aim of monetary and credit control to contrive schemes (discount policies and open market operations) which, by exerting pressures of one sort or another, may induce individuals to refrain from those actions so intimately bound up with the rise and fall of investment, which cause fluctuations in the income stream. But this procedure is only partially effective. It may, therefore, be desirable and possible to offset individual hoarding and dishoarding of money and credit by collective and managed hoarding and dishoarding, and to offset individual extinguishment and

---

[1] It should be noted that the ratio of reserves to deposits is in no way affected by the decline in velocity. The volume of bank deposits is no greater when a hundred-dollar deposit circulates from consumer to retailer, wholesaler and manufacturer than when it lies idle to the credit of the consumer. An idle deposit does not induce the bank to create new bank credit.

creation of bank credit by collective and managed creation and extinguishment of bank credit.

If there is to be a levelling down of purchasing power from the boom period to the depression period, this result can be accomplished only by checking the creation of new purchasing power in boom times or else offsetting these new funds by withholding some part of the purchasing power from the market; and by creating new purchasing power in times of depression or else bringing withheld purchasing power into the market.

There are three faucets through which an increased stream of purchasing power may flow, thereby restoring the depressed income of a community: (1) through producers, in consequence of increased business activity; (2) through consumers, in consequence of the spending of hoards (cash or other forms of idle savings); (3) through the government, in consequence of increased expenditures (such as emergency benefits to the unemployed or public works) financed out of the creation of new credit.[2]

[2] Attention should be called to the fact that when new funds are put in active circulation whether through increased producer activity, or through increased spending of consumer hoards, or through government expenditures, the total community income is likely to be increased by more than the amount originally injected into the market. Money thus thrown into the market runs the complete gamut of production from consumer down through the retailer, wholesaler, and producer at all the various stages of fabrication. Each stage in the process retains a part of the initial expenditure as income. A thousand dollars first injected into the system and passed through all the various stages become finally a thousand dollars of net income for the various persons who coöperated in the whole production process. These persons now find themselves possessed of a thousand dollars of income which they otherwise would not have had. If now they, in turn, make additional purchases the initial thousand dollars start on a new circuit of production and become income for another set of coöperating producers. Thus the injection of new money into the market will raise the money income of the community not by the initial expenditure, but by this amount multiplied by the *income velocity of money*, or the number of times this initial money passes through a related sequence of production in any given period, for example one year.

The income velocity of money is the number of times money passes through a chain of production and again becomes income in a given period of time. Pigou (*The Theory of Unemployment*) estimates that the income velocity of money is about three per annum. This checks with American experience in boom times. Thus, in 1929 the total amount

Under the system of private enterprise and the prevailing financial institutions, the money income of a community is paid out, for the most part, from banks through business entrepreneurs. If business men are optimistic and see prospects of making profits, operations are expanded, idle bank credit is utilized, more money is paid out to labor and the owners of other factors of production, and the purchasing power of the community (in terms of money) is increased. If, on the other hand, owing to unfavorable developments of a non-monetary character—such as the termination of the construction of a transcontinental railroad or of the fixed plant of a new giant industry, the decline of major industries due to technological developments, disturbances to world trade arising from political interferences, or, as is commonly the case, an artificial expansion in the means of production as a whole—the outlook for making profits becomes gloomy, pessimism cumulates among business men, less of the available credit is utilized, less money is paid out to the community, the volume of spendable funds actively functioning in the market is diminished, and a vicious spiral of deflation is started.

In consequence of the world-wide depression the price system has more than ever before been brought to the bar of judgment, and is being widely challenged. Under this

---

of money (cash and deposit currency) was about $30,000,000,000 while the national income was about $90,000,000,000. It follows that the income velocity of money must have been about three per annum. It is important to distinguish sharply the income velocity of money from the *transaction velocity of* money. The latter is obviously many times greater.

During a depression, of course, this newly created income would not all be utilized in further purchases or at least not with the rapidity experienced in good times. At each stage a part would be held idle either in the form of actual cash or of deposits. Very probably the best that could be hoped for is that the injection of a given quantity of money into the market in bad times will increase the money income of a country by an amount equal to twice the new money created. In other words, the income velocity of money in depression is not likely to exceed two and may vary likely not exceed one and one-half.

system, fluctuations in the money income of the community come about chiefly through the rise and fall of investment. The fluctuations of investment, we know from Wicksell, come about, on the one side, through changes in the prospective rate of profit, due in large part to technological developments, and on the other side, through changes in the market rate of interest. If violent changes are taking place in these factors, enormous fluctuations may occur in the output of capital goods and in the money income of the community; and this is likely to bring about profound changes in the price level, in the internal price structure and thence, in turn, in the prospective rate of profit, so that this set of reactions once started tends to develop a cumulative process of economic instability.

The banker-producer bottle-neck is the vital point in the modern price structure. It was the hope of Wicksell, and more recently of Keynes, that unfavorable developments in the *real* phenomena could be offset by a vigorous counteracting monetary policy. If the prospective rate of profit were falling it was thought that by making the terms of lending more favorable, the bottle-neck would not be contracted and producer credit could be made to flow steadily at an undiminished rate.

According to Wicksell, new investment will be undertaken (and therefore purchasing power will increase and prices will rise), if the market rate of interest is pushed below the prospective rate of profit. The flow of purchasing power (and hence the price level) could, he believed, be controlled by adjusting the market rate to the natural (productivity or profit) rate. If the market rate is below the natural rate, prices tend to rise, if above the natural rate, prices tend to fall.

This analysis of tendencies is theoretically sound, but as a practical means of securing a steady flow of purchasing power Wicksell's proposal is quite ineffective. During a depression the prospective rate of profit on new investment is likely to be a minus quantity. In order to bring about an increased flow of purchasing power, therefore, it would be necessary to establish a minus rate of interest in the money and capital markets. This it is not possible to do.

Moreover, the Wicksellian thesis fails to recognize sufficiently the factor of uncertainty in entrepreneurial investment calculations. Under certain conditions the anticipated rate of profit on new investment is subject to numerous uncertainties; while at other times the future appears to be much more dependable. The spirit of enterprise is ruled in large part by the state of confidence. No matter how high the prospective rate of profit, entrepreneurs may still be deterred from making new investment if confronted with numerous uncertainties.

In our view, the monetary mechanism suggested by Wicksell, directed to stabilize the flow of effective purchasing power, cannot alone accomplish the desired result. In the final analysis, the essential problem is that of stabilizing investment in new capital goods, both durable consumers' goods and producers' goods. We know that the rise and fall of activity in the capital goods industries is the essence of prosperity and depression. It is of the utmost importance never to lose sight of this fundamental characteristic of business fluctuations. There is reason to believe (though past experience is none too encouraging) that monetary weapons may be made reasonably effective as a check upon an excessive burst of new capital investment. But once the investment in new capital goods has been overdone, no matter how plentiful the funds for new investment may be made by monetary means, there appears to be little that can be done to bring private investment again to a plane which will restore the purchasing power of the community. One has to wait until depreciation, obsolescence, new inventions, and the development of new products and new industries have done their work. At best, monetary measures can only prepare the soil for the growth of new investment.

Supplementary to monetary measures, aimed at counteracting the loss of business confidence occasioned mainly by non-monetary disturbances, are the inevitable pressures upon costs forced tardily but eventually by unemployment and hard times. Historically this, indeed, is the essential process by which confidence is restored. It is a common fallacy—one which has seriously delayed revival in the current world depression—that cost reduction merely has the effect of causing a further fall in prices, and so an endless spiral of deflation. This view, so widely held by the business community and the general public, rests upon a wholly wrong understanding of the functioning of the modern credit structure and a lack of knowledge of past experience. With a drastic fall in costs, the entrepreneur again begins to feel solid ground under him. Courage to carry on is restored, stocks of commodities are liquidated in smaller volume, some new investments in fixed capital are made, and so the commodity market is improved. It is just the drastic readjustment of costs that operates powerfully to restore confidence and to stop the decline in selling prices.

Expansion of new investment depends not merely upon the rate of interest, but also on the cost of materials and labor. The longer the life of the capital or investment goods, the more significant the rate of interest becomes. But the rate of interest can never be equally as important as the materials and labor costs. In the case of housing, the interest rate accounts normally for about one-half the rental. If the interest rate were cut in two, rents could be reduced by 25 per cent. But if the cost of construction (materials and labor) were cut in two, rents could be reduced by 50 per cent. This is true because the total interest burden depends not only upon the rate of interest but also upon the construction costs. At any assumed rate of interest, the total interest burden will vary proportionally with the cost of construction or the total capital investment.

If the material and labor costs of construction are relatively rigid, as appears to be the case,[3] comparatively slight changes in prices (or rents) may cause violent fluctuations in the prospective rate of profit in new investment. In a period of depression, a drastic reduction in the rate of interest (the Wicksellian remedy) will surely tend to restore a higher level of constructional (investment) activity. But a sharp reduction in the cost of construction (materials and labor) would be even more effective.

Applying the Wicksellian analysis to wage rates, Dr. Jorgen Pedersen of the University of Copenhagen[4] concludes that fluctuations in the flow of effective purchasing power may be traced to the divergence of actual wage rates from natural (or productivity) wage rates. If the actual wage rates are below the natural wage rates, new investment is made, more purchasing power is thereby put in circulation, and prices tend to rise. Thus a revival in business activity may be stimulated. If the actual wage rate is pushed above the natural wage rate, a boom may be checked.

Either one of these proposals (Wicksell's or Pedersen's), if rigorously applied to the limit, would doubtless go far to stabilize purchasing power, prices, profits, and production. Each suffers, however, from the serious defect that it seeks to offset the complex maladjustment in the whole internal price structure by the manipulation of a single

[3] See F. C. Mills, "Aspects of Recent Price Changes," National Bureau of Economic Research, Bulletin 48, October 31, 1933.

[4] Cf. Jorgen Pedersen, "Wicksells Theorie des Zusammenhangs zwischen Zinssatz und Geldwertschwankungen," *Archiv für Sozialwissenschaft und Sozialpolitik*, May, 1933.

cost factor. The interest rate (or the wage rate) is made to take the whole shock of the derangement caused by the failure of the various cost factors to adjust to the changed data. This is the chief difficulty. An arbitrarily severe burden is placed upon one strand in the cost structure. What is needed is to make all costs, or at least the more important ones, flexible.

This could be done by systematic economic planning, by deliberate institutional arrangements. Economic planning need not necessarily run in terms of the fixing of prices and production quotas. This way lies a restriction of output and lower real income. Economic planning can, if we will, be directed toward the creation of a more flexible economic structure, not a more rigid one.

It is a striking fact that the gross money incomes of farmers and of urban wage-earners have declined in like proportion from 1929 to 1933.[5] Urban incomes were influenced by cost rigidity with consequent sharp reduction in industrial output and employment. Rural incomes were affected by sustained output with sharp reduction in prices. If a systematic scheme of cost flexibility could be incorporated into our whole industrial structure so that production in all lines could be sustained, then employment and real income would not suffer the devastating declines which have recently been experienced.

We are not unfamiliar with the system, adopted in many collective agreements, of adjusting money wage rates in accordance with some price index. Such schemes are not inimical to the modern trend of organization. Indeed only on the basis of well developed trade associations and trade unions is the mechanism at hand to build the systematic machinery for an orderly internal adjustment of the cost-price structure.

A large measure of flexibility could be achieved by the

[5] See Evans Clark, *The Internal Debts of the United States*, p. 62.

orderly adjustment of some five or six fundamental cost groups. The following are suggested for consideration: (1) interest charges; (2) depreciation; (3) railroad and public utility rates; (4) basic iron and steel products; (5) taxes; (6) wage rates.

Much research is available on the precise mechanism by which adjustments could be made in a number of basic costs. For others additional work needs to be done. But the problem is far from an impossible one, if we definitely set ourselves the task of deliberately securing, through systematic planning, an orderly scheme of economic flexibility.

Two general measures, therefore, are available to enlarge the stream of purchasing power flowing into the market through the first faucet—that of private enterprise. They are (to sum up): (1) monetary measures (central bank policies operating in the money and capital markets) by means of which the terms of lending are made more favorable, and (2) cost reductions, particularly those which affect the capital-producing industries. Both measures are designed to stimulate new construction and new investment, thereby increasing activity in the field of durable goods, the decline of which is always chiefly responsible for the curtailment of purchasing power.

Yet at best, the stability of investment is, under modern conditions, rendered extraordinarily difficult as a result of: (1) rapid shifts in industry such as those of the last decade, (2) violent disturbances in the international field such as have arisen in the post-War period, (3) the growing importance of durable goods, and (4) the slowing down of the growth factor, due to population stabilization.

In the face of serious disturbances—whether occasioned by rapid changes in technology or by political disorders affecting the industrial intercourse of nations—the confidence of business men is likely to be so shaken, the prospect of a reasonable rate of profit is made so gloomy, that new investment, stimulated by central bank action and cost adjustment, is inadequate to maintain purchasing power. The shocks to which modern capitalism is subject appear to be so great that the gloomy outlook for profit-making cannot be effectively overcome by these means. Either they are not powerful enough, or they operate too slowly. The flow of purchasing power is dammed up before it reaches the consumer, since the entrepreneur has not sufficient confidence in the future to utilize the available credit resources. Thus the banker-producer credit mechanism appears no longer adequate to provide a reasonably steady flow of spendable funds. There is, accordingly, a growing insistence that purchasing power must be transmitted to the consumer through some other channel.

It has been urged, therefore, that the purchasing power of the community should be maintained by opening other faucets—faucets which connect bank credit directly with consumers without the intermediary of the producer. Instead of making consumer purchasing power wholly dependent upon the action of entrepreneurs, it is proposed to invert the relationship—at least in times of emergency—and control producer optimism through the maintenance, by direct methods, of the volume of spendable funds.

In consequence of this striving for stability of purchasing power, however, forces have been set in motion which, unless carefully administered, will tend to intensify the instability of the price structure for capital goods. It is sought (faucet No. 2, for example) to achieve stabilization of consumer income by building up reserves in good times to be drawn upon and distributed in periods of depression.

The first important development in this direction was the accumulation of corporate reserves intended to insure stability of dividend payments to stockholders. This development is of comparatively recent date but by now has assumed fairly large proportions.

In periods of prosperity profits are not distributed in large part but are pumped into the capital market, thereby stimulating an abnormal development of capital formation. And in periods of depression the invested reserves are dumped on the capital market in order to supply the cash needed for dividend payments. Thus the effort to stabilize the incomes of dividend receivers has the effect of lowering the capital market rate in times of prosperity and raising the capital market rate in times of depression. This, in turn, stimulates investment unduly during the boom and retards the return of investment during the depression phase. In other words, the effort to stabilize the incomes of stockholders affects the market rate of interest in a manner precisely opposite to that which Wicksell has so clearly shown is needed to secure stabilization of income and of the price level. The policy of modern corporations, therefore, is in danger of working directly counter to what has by now come to be generally regarded as sound banking policy.

We are now entering a period when other reserves similar in character to dividend reserves are being widely urged and already in large part adopted. I refer to the accumulation of unemployment reserves in good times to be paid out (faucet No. 2) in benefits to the unemployed in periods of depression, and to public finance budgetary arrangements which are intended to make possible the postponement of large public works programs (faucet No. 3) to periods of depression. It makes no difference, from the standpoint of the argument in hand, whether such budgeting of public works is made possible by the accumulation of prosperity reserves to be expended in constructional programs in periods of unemployment, or whether the public works are financed in the depression period by an issue of public bonds to be redeemed in the succeeding period of prosperity. In either event the effect upon the capital market is to reduce the rate of interest in times of pros-

perity and raise it in times of depression. Unless counteracting steps are taken the effect is to stimulate private
investment unduly in the boom period and to retard it in the
depression.

The larger the proportion of the total income available
for expenditure on capital goods, the greater is the *possibility* of violent cyclical fluctuations. The greater the
surplus of a community over and above a bare subsistence
level, the more is it liable to instability. In so far as the
building up of dividend reserves and unemployment reserves (we may call these "Consumers' Reserves") stimulates saving, this presents a danger, but there is another
side to the story. When a country "guarantees" to all its
citizens a decent minimum of subsistence, a bottom is
thereby put to depressions. For a depression is not due to
a lack of purchasing power but rather to a lack of willingness to bring into effective use the purchasing power which
is available. Capital goods need not be purchased when the
outlook is pessimistic, but current liquid consumers' goods
will be purchased in so far as the individuals are able to do
so. If, now, the basic current needs of the unemployed are
definitely maintained by unemployment insurance, the
minimum of purchasing power which will continue to flow
into the market will thereby be raised. [6]

The progressive decline of income during the depression
tends to widen the disparity between income and capital
goods capacity. An excess capacity which may have accumulated toward the end of the boom thereby becomes, in
relation to income, even greater. The decline in income
outruns depreciation. Destitute families crowd together
in small apartments and houses, thereby creating more and
more vacant dwelling space. Unemployment insurance

[6]To be sure, it is always possible that reserve schemes may be so mismanaged that
funds which would otherwise flow into the capital goods industries would be drained
off or dammed up. But this result (as we shall see) is by no means inherent or necessary.

tends to prevent this overcrowding, and thereby helps to put a definite bottom to the decline of residential construction.

With unemployment insurance in the background, the whole wage-earning group feels a sense of security which is quite absent in countries without such safeguards. Where no prohibition against destitution obtains, a fear psychology becomes dominant. Employed workers save a disproportionate part of their income at the very moment when savings can find no outlet in new investment and must therefore "run to waste". Idle savings represent withholding of purchasing power from the commodity market, prices fall, and the total money income in the succeeding period of time is thereby reduced. If a minimum of subsistence were guaranteed, the decline of purchasing power occasioned by this fear psychology could be stopped. Thus such a sustained minimum helps to set a limit to a depression.

It is always possible that new funds injected into the market through the second and third faucets outlined above might cause a contraction of the flow coming out through the first faucet—that of private business activity. Suppose, for example, that the Consumers' Reserves had been invested in bonds, and suppose the liquidation of these bonds (for the purpose of securing cash with which to pay unemployment benefits) caused a deflation of bond values, weakened the capital market, and made still more pessimistic the outlook for investment. In this event the money injected into the market through the second faucet might be offset by a contraction of the flow of funds through the first faucet. Worse yet, there would be no assurance that the money drawn from the second faucet was really *new* money. It might have been drained off from the income stream flowing through the first faucet. It would be new money only when it was drawn from idle funds or from newly created bank credit.

The manner in which reserve funds are administered is therefore a consideration of utmost importance. The payment of unemployment benefits, for example, increases the stream of purchasing power which flows through the second faucet. This is a direct gain, but one must be careful that the funds are not so administered that the stream from the first faucet is either drained off or blocked.

The administration of Consumers' Reserve Funds may be viewed either as a substitute for Federal Reserve control of credit, or else as a supplement thereto. The new machinery might become a *substitute* either through abolition of the Federal Reserve System, or because the funds were so managed that the Federal Reserve System would become helpless in the face of the new rival and lose all control of the situation. The latter eventuality is, however, scarcely likely if the provision of the Thomas Amendment to the farm relief act, giving discretionary powers to the Reserve Board, with the approval of the President, to raise or lower the reserve requirements of member banks, is continued in force. If, on the other hand, the new system should become a *supplement* to Federal Reserve control, it would be a question of policy with the Federal Reserve Board whether to attempt to offset the actions of the administrators of the Consumers' Reserve Funds, or to ignore them, or to be guided by them in an endeavor to coöperate.

We are not justified in making the assumption that the action of the Federal Reserve Banks would in no way be affected by the introduction of the Consumers' Reserve Funds. Indeed, under the Federal Reserve Act the Reserve Banks are charged with the responsibility of regulating the credit supply "with a view to accommodating commerce and business". It can no longer be said that the expansion and contraction of bank credit are controlled, as under a more laissez-faire system, by the quantity of gold and lawful money. Even in the boom of 1928-29, the limits of possible expansion were far from reached. The restrictions imposed upon credit expansion by the Federal Reserve Board during this period were instituted for reasons having to do with the broader aspects of economic stability, such as the accommodation of business as against speculation, and not because the extreme limits of credit expansion had been reached.

It is, therefore, likely that, whatever action is taken by the administrators of the Consumers' Reserve Funds, the Federal Reserve Board must maintain an independent judgment as to the amount of credit expansion needed to accommodate business in view of the general situation. The Reserve System might therefore be compelled to step in and counteract the operations of the Consumers' Funds unless, indeed, these operations happened to coincide with the wishes of the Federal Reserve Board.

But if the weapons of the Reserve System are, in fact, inadequate to achieve the ends sought, and if the new machinery should provide additional means of control which automatically or by conscious volition might tend to produce the desired results, then the Federal Reserve authorities should welcome the Consumers' Reserve mechanism. Quite possibly, however, the administration of the Consumers' Funds, particularly at certain phases of the cycle, might vitiate the control policy of the Reserve Banks either by going directly counter to it or by carrying the desired movement too far.

It is proposed in the brief discussion which follows to consider various possible procedures in the administration of Consumers' Reserves. These funds might be administered by any one of the following methods:

(1) The funds might be placed in deposits (a) with com-

mercial banks; (b) with Federal Reserve Banks; (c) with savings banks.

(2) The funds might be invested in commercial paper or short term obligations of the Federal government purchased in the open market.

(3) The funds might be invested in United States government bonds (a) purchased and sold in the open market; (b) purchased from and sold to the Federal Reserve Banks; (c) purchased from and sold to the United States Treasury.

(4) The funds might be kept either in whole or in part in money hoards.

What are the comparative merits of the various methods of administering Consumers' Reserve Funds?

Consider the relative merits of placing the Consumers' Reserves in demand deposits with commercial banks on the one side, and in savings accounts on the other. In both cases the use of this method would tend to curtail the volume of the effective money supply during the period of prosperity. The demand deposits method has the advantage in checking the boom, since this method would clearly compel bankers to carry a higher reserve ratio than the savings account method. Fear has been expressed that in the period of depression the withdrawal of deposits would force liquidation of bank assets. But since these funds would for the most part at once find their way into the consumers' markets they would quickly turn up as new deposits somewhere in the banking system. Countering any deflationary tendencies, therefore, is the new purchasing power which the payment of dividends and unemployment benefits brings into the market.

Consider next the comparative merits of the placement of Consumers' Reserves in demand deposits with commercial banks in contrast with the investment of these Funds in short-term maturities. Both of these methods tend to check the expansion of the effective money supply during the boom period, the former because *the banks will wish to carry a larger cash reserve against the unemployment reserve deposits*, and the latter because it encroaches upon the available secondary reserve, thus necessitating the carrying of a larger primary reserve. The likelihood is that the former method will impose a greater restraint upon bank credit expansion than the latter. On the other hand, both methods appear to offer equal advantages in the maintenance of purchasing power during the depression.

If we compare the merits of the savings deposit method with the method of investment in Federal bonds (the purchases and sales being made by the Consumers' Reserve Funds in the open market) we obtain the following results: the former method imposes some restraint upon the expansion of the effective money supply during the boom period by forcing upon the banks the policy of carrying a somewhat larger cash reserve; the latter method appears to impose no restraints upon the volume of bank credit in this phase of the cycle. During the depression phase both methods involve the liquidation of bonds. The effect on bond prices will be the same in either case. The advantage is, however, with the former method (that of savings deposits) because this procedure involves liquidation of assets owned by the banks progressively as the depression deepens. Should this liquidation cause a depreciation of bonds, it is evident that the banks will lose less by unloading their assets and paying off the Consumers' Reserve deposits than would be the case under the second method where the liquidation of bonds is made by the Consumers' Reserve Funds. In this latter case, the banks not having to pay off deposits to the Consumers' Reserve Funds would presumably find themselves at the end of the depression period with a larger volume of both deposit obligations and bonds than would be the case under the first method; but they would suffer at the close of the depression the full measure of the bond depreciation, whereas, under the former method, this depreciation would have been minimized by the forced sale of bonds from time to time during the depression period before the full effect of the liquidation had affected bond prices.

Compare next the method of placing the Consumers' Reserves in demand deposits in the Federal Reserve Banks with the method of bond purchase from and sale to the Federal Reserve Banks by the Consumers' Reserve Funds. Under the former method, when the Consumers' Reserve Funds make deposits with the Federal Reserve Banks, the sums are transferred from member bank balances in the Federal Reserve Banks to the new accounts, and the reserves of the member banks are thereby reduced. On the other hand, when the Consumers' Reserve Funds withdraw deposits, the Federal Reserve Banks pay out drafts to the Funds. These drafts are then deposited with member banks which in turn send them back to the Federal Reserve Banks for collection. The ultimate effect is that member banks' reserves are built up. Both methods serve to contract and expand member bank reserves. Both methods therefore tend to stabilize the effective money supply. There is, however, the notable difference that under the former method the deposit liabilities and assets of Federal Reserve Banks are kept intact, the only effect of this procedure being to transfer a part of the deposits of member banks with the Federal Reserve to the Consumers' Reserve Funds. Under the latter method, however, (that of bond purchase from and sale to the Federal Reserve Banks) the effect is to force a somewhat violent fluctuation in the deposit liabilities and assets of the Federal Reserve Banks. The effect of the former method is to stabilize the total resources and liabilities of the Reserve System, at the same time making possible as large variations in member bank reserves as are produced by the latter method. Neither method insures an appropriate adjustment of member bank reserves to the stabilization program. The operations are, moreover, on a scale so large that without counteracting action by the Federal Reserve Banks, the contraction imposed upon bank credit expansion during the prosperity phase would be far too great. Under either method, therefore, the Federal Reserve System would be forced to take steps to modify and adjust the arbitrary influence of the accumulation of Consumers' Reserves.

Compare next the method of purchase and sale of bonds from and to the Federal Reserve Banks with the method of purchase and sale from and to the United States Treasury. The latter method relieves the Federal Reserve Banks of the necessity of loading up their portfolios with an excessive quantity of government bonds. The Treasury Department instead purchases those bonds and issues against them legal tender notes. This relief of the Federal Reserve Banks is, as is well known, the ground on which Senator Glass predicated his remark that the greenback proposal in the Thomas Amendment to the farm relief act was less objectionable than the open market proposal. Against this advantage is the obvious objection that it would pump into circulation, periodically, large quantities of legal tender notes.

Consider now the relative merits of the hoarding method with the method of buying bonds from and selling them to the Federal Reserve System. The hoarding method puts a powerful restraint upon bank credit expansion during the boom period—so much so indeed, that, if used to the limit, it would endanger the power of the Federal Reserve System to control the situation. If, however, the hoarding is placed under the control of the Federal Reserve Banks, the method becomes a mere formality. The alternative method, in contrast, merely reinforces, and makes more effective, open-market operations.

Consider finally the comparative merits of the hoarding method with the placement of the Consumers' Reserves in the form of demand deposits with the Federal Reserve Banks. If the hoards assumed entirely the form of gold and lawful money, the effect is clearly to denude the Federal Reserve System of its cash resources. This the demand deposit method does not do. The hoarding method in short reduces the reserves of the Federal Reserve Banks; the demand deposit method reduces the reserves of the member banks. The restraining effect of the hoarding method is therefore enormously greater than that of the demand deposit method. If the hoards consist of Federal Reserve notes, the restraining effect is minimized considerably since Federal Reserve notes represent only 40 per cent in gold.

The eight methods considered may be placed in four categories as follows:

(1) Those methods which would produce a violent fluctuation in the reserves of the Federal Reserve Banks themselves.

Only one of the eight methods falls in this category—that of placing the Consumers' Reserve Funds in cash hoards. Obviously any method which expands and contracts the reserves of the central banks is the most powerful in its influence on the credit structure. As a method of credit control, it not only competes with the Federal Reserve Banks but it may be said to threaten its very basis. This method would indeed be so powerful that it would well-nigh usurp the throne and oust the Federal Reserve Bank from control.

(2) Those methods which would produce a fluctuation in the surplus reserves of the member banks.

Three of the eight methods discussed above fall in this category. They are as follows: (a) deposit of Consumers' Reserve Funds with Federal Reserve Banks; (b) investment

of Consumers' Reserve Funds in bonds purchased from and
sold to the Federal Reserve Banks; (c) exchange of Consumers' Reserve investments against United States notes.

Each of these methods would result in an expansion or
contraction, as the case may be, of member bank reserves.
This procedure would therefore perform a function hitherto
entrusted, since the inauguration of the Federal Reserve
System, exclusively to the Federal Reserve Banks. It makes
the Consumers' Reserve Funds direct competitors of the
Federal Reserve Banks in the control of credit.

(3) Those methods which tend to affect the reserve
requirements of the member banks, not by automatically
increasing the member bank reserves, but by forcing the
member banks to carry a larger reserve in view of the character of their liabilities or because of encroachment upon
secondary reserves.

Of the eight methods considered the following three fall
in this category. They would tend to affect the reserve
ratio, with a magnitude in the order given below: (a) funds
placed in demand deposits with commercial banks;
(b) funds placed in savings deposits; (c) funds invested in
short term maturities.

(4) Those methods which appear to have no influence
upon either the volume of reserves or reserve requirements.

One method alone of the eight appears to fall in this
category. It is that method under which Consumers' Reserve Funds are invested in bonds purchased and sold in the
open market.

There is perhaps danger of getting lost in minutiae.
Broadly considered, what is needed, if we are to sustain a
fairly even flow of purchasing power, is to open the second
faucet when the first one dries up. This means that as fast
as producers' credit is contracted (bank loans being liquidated in consequence of reduced business activity) new
bank credit will be created through increased investment

in the assets formerly owned by the Consumers' Reserve Funds. To illustrate: the loans of all member banks declined from $26.2 billion in October 1929 to $12.9 billion in June 1933, while investments increased from $9.7 billion to $11.9 billion. While there was some slight offset on the side of investments to the decline in loans this was far from adequate.

It would make little difference in the final analysis whether the commercial banks bought the additional investments directly from the Dividend and Unemployment Reserve Funds or from savings banks with which the Reserve Funds had been deposited. By and large the fundamental facts are the same whether or not the savings banks come in as intermediaries between the Consumers' Reserve Funds and the ultimate investment of these Funds in suitable obligations. What is important is that bank credit shall not decline, and this could be accomplished by substituting investment for loans as business activity diminished. The increased flow of bank credit to consumers would thus offset the diminished flow to producers.

In effect the industrial system would set itself the task of maintaining a fairly even flow of dividend and wage payments whether business was active or not. When times were good, the commercial banks would be relieved of a portion of their investment portfolio, leaving them free to put funds in loans to finance increased business activity. When times were bad the banks would be called upon to take on more investments, and this they would be quite able to do owing to the diminished business demands for bank credit. In effect, as business activity declined and credit to producers diminished, the banks would step into the breach and supply the funds with which to maintain wage and dividend payments by exchanging consumer credit for the assets of Dividend and Unemployment Reserve Funds. The total volume of bank credit would thereby be

measurably sustained. When business was good, the bulk
of the total volume would flow out to the community
through credit advanced to the producer; when business
was bad, producer credit would decline, and relatively
more would be paid out directly to consumers through advances made on investments previously accumulated by
Consumers' Reserve Funds.

Except for the phenomenon of cash hoarding by deposi-
tors there appears to be no good reason why banks should
not be able to offset a decline in loans by increased investments. The elimination of cash hoarding awaits the development of a thoroughly sound banking system. This is
an absolutely necessary prerequisite for the maintenance of
purchasing power. It is, however, probable that even
though hoarding is eliminated, the banks will find it
expedient in periods of low business activity to maintain
larger cash balances. To the extent that this is the case, in
order to maintain a constant level of bank credit, it would
be necessary for the Federal Reserve Banks, through open
market operations, to supply the banks with the requisite
surplus cash balances. Thus the Reserve Banks would indirectly help to bolster up the market for the assets of the
Consumers' Reserve Funds.

But there would always be the danger that the member
banks would not take all the funds offered by the Dividend
and Unemployment Reserve Funds. To make sure that the
market would be well sustained and that the needed cash
resources would really be obtained from new credit (and
not simply drained off from current income) it might prove
desirable, if indeed, not necessary, to establish a new
Federal bank which would be prepared to purchase these
securities. Such a bank should, in common with member
banks, have at its disposal the resources of the Federal
Reserve System.

The serious difficulty which the modern industrial system encounters in the effort to maintain purchasing power in the face of declining business activity is the lack of avenues through which credit may be put directly into the hands of consumers. Only as really large Consumers' Reserve Funds are built up can this be accomplished.

Yet even though such funds should eventually be built up in large volume, there would never be any assurance that they would be adequate or would not eventually be drained dry. There must therefore always be in the background the third faucet—that of Federal expenditures through public works and emergency benefits to the unemployed, supplemental to state unemployment insurance systems.

The great merit of the development of Consumers' Reserve Funds on a large scale, in contrast to public expenditures, is that they offer a means by which purchasing power can be got out into the community without placing a severe strain on the public treasury. The third faucet (public expenditures) has the great demerit that the funds it pours out tend to exhaust the public credit and constitute a levy on the future.

The accumulation of Consumers' Reserve Funds may, of course, have the effect of raising (at least in times of prosperity) the ratio of saving to spending. It has been suggested by some economists that the net effect of reduced spending would be a lower price level of consumers' goods than would otherwise have been the case, and that, in consequence, the stimulus to investment in fixed capital would thereby tend to be minimized. This view is, however, incorrect and is based on a confusion of the effect on capital formation of (1) higher or lower prices of consumers' goods, and (2) a change in the rate of interest. It is true that in consequence of the decreased spending and increased saving, consumers' prices would be low relative to the prices of producers' goods. But this, in effect, means a lower rate of interest, and a lower rate of interest stimulates an expansion of capital investment in fields which at higher rates would be unprofitable. It is not the absolute height of the price level of consumers' goods which is determining. It is the relation of the level of consumers' goods prices to the prices of producers' goods, or, in other words, the rate of interest that determines the volume of capital investment.[7] Put in another way, there is no sound reason to suppose that the total volume of purchasing power would necessarily be contracted in the prosperity period by the assumed decline in spending and increase in saving. On the other hand, the total volume of bank credit could be kept within the bounds of reasonable stability despite the assumed tendency toward a relative increase in capital formation. Nor would the increase of capital accumulations necessarily lead to an undue expansion of producers' goods, since savings might as well find an outlet in durable consumers' goods. Moreover, we need not feel any particular alarm at a moderate expansion of capital goods production occasioned by an increase in real saving.[8] The essentially unhealthy characteristic of all booms is the stimulus given to capital formation by an undue expansion of bank credit. But this is subject to central bank control, and is in no sense a necessary counterpart of the accumulation of Consumers' Reserve Funds.

The building up of Consumers' Reserve Funds tends to lower the rate of interest and therefore to increase the volume of investment in new capital. But this tendency may be counteracted by monetary policy intended to raise the rate of interest. Thus, the development of Consumers' Reserve Funds does not of necessity result in the excessive expansion of capital goods. The scheme only means that

[7]See Alvin H. Hansen and Herbert Tout, "Investment and Saving in Business Cycle Theory", *Econometrica*, April 1933.

[8]See F. A. Hayek, *Prices and Production*.

a part of the investment goods produced is financed by funds accumulated by Consumers' Reserves. In the depression period these Reserve Funds provide a resisting wall to hold back the receding tide of deflation. The net effect need not be to stimulate unduly the activity of the capital goods industries in the boom, but will rather serve to maintain a higher rate of activity in both consumers' and producers' goods industries during the depression.[9]

For once it is recognized that in mid-slump the speedy restoration of full activity in the instrumental trades is in any case out of the question, the alleged objections to the maintenance of consumption at the maximum level seem to crumble away. Under such conditions a policy of reflation designed to maintain the purchasing power of consumers seems to contain little danger of a pernicious "warping of the structure of production"; and at the same time to offer the best hope of eventually restoring "rentability" to the capital structure left stranded by the receding tide.[10]

It may, of course, be admitted at once that all programs of stabilization should concentrate on the prevention of the boom,[11] hoping thereby to forestall maladjustments and thus stave off, as far as may be, the depression. Nevertheless, with the best of intentions and institutional control we can be certain that maladjustments, in a progressive society, will develop in greater or less degree. How to prevent past maladjustments, however caused, from running riot and developing into a cumulated spiral of deflation—this is the problem which we must necessarily

[9]The essential point is that the Consumers' Reserves provide a basis for the expansion of money directly to consumers. The method suggested is admittedly more clumsy than outright fiat money, but it is much safer.

[10]D. A. Robertson, "Der Stand und die nächste Zukunft der Konjunkturforschung", *Festschrift für Arthur Spiethoff*, 1933.

[11]But if we are to lop off the boom we must frankly face the unpleasant fact that our capital goods industries, inflated by the artificial stimuli of the boom, are overexpanded. Either we must set ourselves the trying task of deflating the investment goods industries along with agriculture, or else we must deliberately raise sufficient public revenues to fill up the gap through a large and permanent expansion of public works. To accomplish this end it might even be necessary, at least in some countries, to resort to sales taxes.

face. We must recognize that while every effort needs to be directed toward *prevention*, we must also learn, if possible, to *check the spread* of the disease, once the patient is affected. Instead of permitting the disturbances in special branches of industry to spread to the whole economy like a deadly poison, they should, as far as possible, be localized. A new balance could be built up through the maintenance of the totality of monetary purchasing power without passing through a general deflation. The adjustments that would have to be made before a new equilibrium could be reached would be facilitated through the stimulus given in this manner to the rapid development of those industries the expansion of which is called for by the new conditions. It is a common fallacy of many economists to suppose that deflation is the necessary medium through which the new balance is reached. What is needed is a *transfer of factors*, and this can most speedily be effected by safeguarding the general purchasing power.

Business enterprises cannot be responsible for the maintenance of purchasing power. Self-preservation and continuance of private enterprise demand that they look to the profit margin. It is gradually coming to be recognized, however, that it is a responsibility of the central banks to prevent, as far as possible, general collapse of purchasing power. Yet it is doubtful, as we have seen, whether they can perform this function alone, without the aid of Consumers' Reserve Funds and of the government. It may be that we have reached a stage in the development of modern industry in which free enterprise and the price system cannot continue to function unless we develop new institutions, in coöperation with the central banks, to safeguard the maintenance of *purchasing power as a whole*. Without this, in a state of general collapse of producer confidence, each entrepreneur in self-defense contracts his operations—a policy which, if pursued by all, is suicidal to the general economy.

It is becoming a serious question whether modern communities can escape the dilemma either of undertaking the maintenance of total purchasing power (leaving private initiative to carry on the great bulk of economic activities) or else of taking over the operation of all enterprise itself.

What is needed is the guarantee that industry *as a whole* shall not suffer losses by reason of those changes arising from the failure of the central banks to maintain purchasing power. This does not mean to guarantee each individual business against loss. If this were done, it would spell the end of the system of private enterprise, the very essence of which is that each business must undertake the risks involved, win profits if possible, but assume the losses if any are incurred. If the government guaranteed each business against loss it would of necessity have to assume control of management. If, however, the total purchasing power of the community could be maintained, though individual businesses would suffer losses, profits would not disappear *en masse* in the whole system.

Unfortunately, any proposal directed to this end is fraught with economic difficulties and, frequently, political dangers, particularly in modern democracies which have so often demonstrated a lack of capacity in self-control. But whether we turn to a planned economy (capitalistic, socialistic, or communistic), or to a regulated price system, a high order of political wisdom and efficiency is essential to success.

# ADDENDUM

## Statement by Josef A. Schumpeter

Any careful reader will, I believe, find in the report, expressly or implicitly, by proposition or qualification, all or nearly all the elements of the economic problem confronting modern society in all industrial countries. If the following remarks express any difference of opinion at all it is a difference of emphasis only, which of course may imply considerable difference in applications to public policy.

(1) Whilst whole-heartedly agreeing with the argument about the pivotal importance, in crises, of government expenditure on public works, and especially on direct relief for the unemployed, I am disposed to lay greater stress on the necessity of not letting budgets go entirely to pieces, and of upholding the principles of careful and conscientious administration of public finances, to which it may be practically impossible to return when once the spirit of reckless expenditure has been allowed to grow up. I also wish to add that taxation itself may be made a useful instrument of remedial policy if taxes which are in any way proportional to business success are systematically lowered in depression and increased in prosperity, in which case they would act in a way similar to that of the variations of the rate of interest.

(2) Although I think the conclusions of the report to be theoretically correct about the most desirable course to take in the matter of monetary policy, I yet agree with Professor Angell that a definite return to the gold standard at the earliest possible moment, without regard to the action of other nations, is the wisest step for the United States to take. If this be not done, serious business will

be unwilling to venture on what otherwise would be its normal course. The pressure of inflationary interests, of which the symptoms are already obvious, may at any moment become irresistible, and situations may arise in which inflation would seem to many people unavoidable. While fully recognizing the weight of the argument of the report, I therefore disagree with Recommendations 2 and 3. As for Conclusion 7, I think that the qualification contained in the second sentence expresses the meaning better than the proposition contained in the first.

(3) We probably differ from one another as to how far the evidence "pointing to a relative failure even in times reputed prosperous to make the most effective and economical use of the capacity for production" is conclusive. With due respect for the high authority of the opinions on which this finding rests, there seems to be room for doubt whether the sources of those errors to which such statements are as a rule exposed have been sufficiently removed. But accepting for the sake of argument the fact, and even the quantitative estimate of its importance, and waiving discussion of all the cases in which temporary but also lasting "over-capacity" is an unavoidable incident of progress, we should be more careful to prevent our readers from overlooking three other facts.

First: insufficient utilization of productive capacity notwithstanding, the increase under the existing system of the real income of *all* classes, during the last thirty years and in spite of the prodigious waste of the War period, will of course be judged by every one according to the standard he applies. But it certainly is not in the nature of an argument against the system. And the inference is not unreasonable that in another thirty years the system, if it were allowed to work on, would produce a national real income such as might make economic care, at least in this country, a thing of the past. As compared with the untried possibilities of planning, this possibility seems to deserve more attention than is usually bestowed on it.

Second: however desirable full and prompt utilization, especially of new productive capacities, may be in some respects, it should not be forgotten that temporarily it would make depressions and unemployment worse, because the disturbance of economic equilibrium by the impact of new products would be still more intense. Some of those sectors of economic life of the inefficiency of which we are in the habit of complaining, such as the wasteful apparatus of distribution, are the very haven in which those whom progress displaces take refuge.

Third: in discussing the advantages of planning, we must look at its probable results in the same realistic spirit in which we look at the shortcomings of the existing system. It then becomes of ominous importance that the attempts at planning of which we have empirical knowledge are in some cases indeed adequately described by the felicitous phrase of this report as trying to solve the great paradox of poverty in the midst of plenty by removing the plenty, while the results in other cases, especially in the case of the Russian experiment, are obviously far below what even a most backward and largely pre-capitalist system would by this time have done for the welfare of the masses. Moreover, if planning is to be undertaken on a large scale within the framework of present society, very difficult questions of organization will arise, about which people will differ according to the degree of confidence they have in the working of the political institutions of their countries, but which must be more satisfactorily settled than they now are.  Failing this, planned economy, however correct theoretically its design may be, is in danger of combining all the worst features of the present system and of socialism, without any of their redeeming points.

(4) Under the influence of temporary vicissitudes, largely

due to extra-economic causes, the desirability of "economic stability" has been greatly overstressed, even where the much abused term has not become synonymous with resistance to socially desirable adaptation. None of the elements the stabilization of which has in turn been clamored for can be stabilized without serious harm to the working of the system. I believe that the report recognizes this, and I also agree fully with its proposition that raising money incomes in response to the increase of the physical volume of production is a feasible alternative to an equivalent fall in the price level. Both methods ultimately attain the same end: increase in real incomes and dissemination of the fruits of progress among all classes. Theoretically (and psychologically) I perfectly appreciate the advantage it would be to make this process obvious by measuring the growing child in an invariant unit of measurement instead of keeping the number of the dollar-inches constant and letting their size or purchasing power grow instead. But, as I believe the practical difficulties of this plan to be greater and the practical disadvantages of the other course to be smaller than my colleagues seem to believe, I will merely echo the sentiments expressed by Professor Mitchell in the second paragraph of his statement.

# INDEX

# INDEX